ANSWERS TO PRAYER

ANSWERS TO PRAYER

GEORGE MUELLER

From
George F. Müeller's Narratives

BL BRIDGE
LOGOS

Alachua, Florida 32615

Bridge-Logos
Alachua, FL 32615 USA

Answers To Prayer
George F. Müeller

Scripture Quotations are from the King James Version of the Bible

Printed in the United States of America.

Library of Congress Catalog Card Number: Pending
International Standard Book Number 978-1-61036-102-6

Compiled and Edited by
Beverlee J. Chadwick
Senior Editor, Bridge Logos, Inc.

VP 02-15-13

TABLE OF CONTENTS

ANSWERS TO PRAYER

FOREWORD

"That the trial of your faith, being much more precious than of gold that perisheth, though it be tried with fire, might be found unto praise and honour and glory at the appearing of Jesus Christ." 1 Peter 1:7

"Open thy mouth wide, and I will fill it." Psalm 81:10

GOD chose for this faith dependent, God called ministry an unbelieving, undisciplined, self-willed, young man, born in 1805, in a country called Prussia now known as Germany.

There will be no cause for doubt in the mind of any reader of the truth of God's promises to every believer after reading the life and ministry of George Müeller.

He was brought up to receive the desires of his heart, whether given to him by his doting father or sinfully obtained by his own hand, that is, until God, the heavenly Potter, got hold of him and began molding, firing, and shaping him into the vessel of His will for his life and lifework that God planned for him.

The time of molding, firing, and shaping was difficult and intense for young George Müeller but necessary. His undisciplined and rebellious heart was soon softened by the Word of God and working of the Holy Spirit and his stubborn self-will became humbled and turned to God's will only in every aspect of his life and ministry.

God taught George Müeller early in his ministry that He alone was the God who heard and answered prayer; He alone was the Provider of everything needed for the work, and He alone received the glory, thanksgiving, and praise from the grateful heart of George Müeller.

The first part of this book, *The Biography of George*

Müeller, relates the mighty workings of God in his life and preparation for this ministry of total trust and faith in God's Word alone. God showed him that by prayer, and his faith and trust in Him alone, that He would supply all the needs of the orphans; the orphan homes, the staff, the Scriptural Knowledge Institute, Missions, and the Müeller family.

The second part, *Answers to Prayer,* will bless in abundance the minds, hearts and spirits of the readers and encourage all who read it in their own walk with God, and to trust Him solely in whatever way He chooses to provide their needs.

The amazing provisions in answer to the times of trial will bless and encourage even the most hesitant soul to heed the Scriptures; the drawing of the Holy Spirit and to launch out into a life of total trust, and confidence in God and His Word.

God does not change, God cannot change. The promises and provisions He made for George Müeller, He will do for all His children who believe and obey His Word. *"Now unto Him that is able to do exceeding abundantly above all that we ask or think, according to the power that worketh in us"* (Ephesians 3:20).

The Wise Sayings of George Müeller are gems to be read, meditated on, and applied as the Holy Spirit directs. What struck me deeply as I worked on this book was the well-known fact that God's Word never changes; the only change that will come about is in us, for we were created to be changed into His image. God's Word, is the foundation and standard for every generation. We need only to believe… and there will be no cause for doubt in the mind of any reader of the truth of God's promises to every believer after reading the life and ministry of George Müeller.

Be prepared to have your prayer life deepened; your faith increased, your understanding of God's Word expanded, and your prayers heard and answered.

*"If ye abide in me, and my words abide in you,
ye shall ask what ye will,
and it shall be done unto you."* John 15:7

Beverlee J. Chadwick
Senior Editor, Bridge Logos Inc.

PREFACE

M R. BROOKS, in this compilation, has endeavored to select those incidents and practical remarks from Mr. Müeller's Narratives, that show in an unmistakable way, both to believers and unbelievers, the secret of believing prayer, the manifest hand of a living God, and His unfailing response, in His own time and way, to every petition which is according to His will.

The careful perusal of these extracts will thus further the great object which Mr. Müeller had in view, without the necessity of reading through the various details of his "Narratives," details which Mr. Müeller felt bound to give when writing periodically the account of God's dealings with him.

For those who have the opportunity, an examination of the "Autobiography of George Müeller, or, a Million and a Half in Answer to Prayer" will richly repay the time spent upon it.

Mr. Müeller's permission for the compilation of this volume is shown in the accompanying facsimile, in the following words: "If the extracts are given exactly as printed, and the punctuation exactly as in the book and in the connection in which the facts stand, I have no objection."

Important Dates in George Müeller's Life

▸ **September 27, 1805:** George Müeller was born in Kroppenstaedt near Halberstadt, Prussia.

▸ **1819:** His mother died when he was fourteen years of age.

▸ **1821:** He was imprisoned for a short time at the age of sixteen for theft.

▸ **1827:** Müeller became a student of divinity at the University of Halle.

▸ **November, 1825:** The Bible study that turned his life to Christ.

▸ **August 27, 1826:** His first sermon.

▸ **August-September 1826:** He spent two life-changing months in A. H. Francke's Orphan House.

▸ **June 13, 1828:** He was accepted provisionally by the London Missionary Society.

▸ **March 19, 1829:** Müeller arrived in London to study at the London Missionary Society.

▸ **August, 1829:** He learned the doctrines of grace while staying in Teignmouth.

▸ **January, 1830:** Müeller's connection with the London Missionary Society was dissolved.

▸ **1830-1832:** He became the stated preacher at Ebenezer Chapel, Teignmouth.

▸ **1830:** Müeller was baptized by immersion.

▸ **October 7, 1830:** Married to Mary Groves.

▸ **October, 1830:** He gave up his salary at his church and for the rest of his life.

▸ **August 9, 1831:** Mary gave birth to a stillborn child.

▸ **May, 1832:** He left Teignmouth to take up ministry in Bristol.

- **July 6, 1832:** Began preaching at Bethesda Chapel with Henry Craik in Bristol.

- **September 17, 1832:** Their daughter, Lydia, was born.

- **February 20, 1834:** He founded the Scripture Knowledge Institute.

- **March 19, 1834:** Their son, Elijah, was born.

- **June 26, 1835:** Son, Elijah, died at one year and five months.

- **November 28, 1836:** The first orphan house was opened.

- **June 13, 1838:** A second stillborn child was born.

- **October 7, 1838:** Müeller's only brother died.

- **March 30, 1840:** His father died.

- **January 22, 1866:** Henry Craik died.

- **February 6, 1870:** His first wife, Mary, died.

- **November 16, 1871:** James Wright, Müeller's successor married Lydia.

- **November 30, 1871:** Müeller remarried. His second wife was Susannah Grace Sangar.

- **January 10, 1890:** His daughter, Lydia, died at the age of 58.

- **January 13, 1895:** Second wife, Susannah, died. He conducted her service at age 90.

- **Thursday, March 10, 1898:** George Müeller died of heart failure at the age of 93, having led a prayer meeting the night before.

- **Monday, March 14, 1898:** George Müeller was buried with his wives, Mary, and Susannah.

BIOGRAPHY OF
GEORGE MÜELLER

Chapter 1

HIS BIRTH AND NEW BIRTH

GEORGE MÜELLER was truly a gift of God to the Church and to the world, yet, he was a man of like passions, and tempted in all points as we are.

He proved for himself and for all others who read this book, that, to those who are willing to take God at His Word and yield themselves to His will, God will do the same and more in their lives. For He is *the same yesterday, and today and for ever.*

The biography of George Müeller may be best studied by dividing it into certain marked periods.

1. From his birth to his new birth or conversion: 1805 – 1825 = 20 years.
2. From his conversion to full entrance on his life work: 1825 – 1835 = 10 years.
3. From this point to the period of his mission tours: 1835 – 1875 = 40 years.
4. From the beginning to the close of these tours: 1875 – 1892 = 17 years.
5. From the close of his tours to his death: 1892 – 1898 = 6 years.

Each period of time is marked by certain conspicuous characteristic features which serve to distinguish it and make its lessons particularly important and memorable.

George Müeller's full name was Johann Georg Ferdinand Müeller; he was born to Johann Friedrich Müeller and Sophie Eleonore Müeller in Kroppenstaedt, Kingdom of Prussia, on September 27, 1805. Prussia is now Kroppenstaedt, Germany.

George did not have the benefit of any parental training whatsoever. His father did favor him over his brother which naturally created jealously and strife between the brothers. Their father gave them money very freely in the hope they would learn how to use it and save it, however, this indulgence resulted in a careless waste of money and opened the doors to a childhood of disobedience, which was the source of many of George's childish sins.

A Life of Lies and Stealing

When his father asked him for an accounting of the money he gave him, George lied to him. Even before he reached 10 years of age he had learned to systematically deceive his father by putting false entries in the record book of what he had received from his father, how he had spent it, and what he had on hand. When his father discovered the truth, the punishment did not stop him nor reform him but led him to more ingenious forms of trickery and fraud. Young George Müeller did not believe his life of stealing and lies was sinful; the only thing that bothered him was having his thieving and lies found out.

A large amount of government funds were entrusted to his father's care, and when some of the money was missing his father became suspicious and set a snare for him. He counted out a portion of the money and hid it where he knew George would find it, and sure enough George took it and hid it under his foot inside his shoe. Knowing his son had found the money, his father searched him and found the money and that made it clear to him that George was no doubt responsible for monies missing in the past.

His Father's Response

Therefore, in an effort to gain help for his wayward child, George's father decided that he should be educated as a clergyman. It seems incredible that such a boy would be deliberately sent to school for a sacred office and calling by his father who knew well his immoral character. However, where a state church exists, the ministry of the Gospel is apt to be treated as a human profession rather than a divine vocation. That lowers the standards of fitness to a low secular level with the main object being making a living, frequently independent of holy living.

So, at the age of 11 he was sent off to the Cathedral Classical School in Halberstadt for his primary education before his entrance into a university. Unfortunately, the school had no positive influence on him, instead He learned to drink, gamble, and various other indulgences. When he was 14, his mother lay dying in her bed as her boy of 14 was drunk and reeling through the streets; even her death had no influence on his sinful life.

He continued his education and his sinful life throughout his teen years. In spite of his wayward life, he was not only admitted to honorable standing as a university student, but accepted as a candidate for holy orders with permission to preach in the Lutheran establishment. He knew absolutely nothing about God, salvation or the gospel of saving grace.

THE DRAWING OF THE HOLY SPIRIT ON HIS LIFE

One Saturday afternoon in the middle of November, 1825, George and a friend were returning from a walk when his friend said he was going to a meeting that evening at a believer's house. A small group of friends met to sing, pray, and read the Word of God and a printed sermon. This was not what Müeller normally did on Saturday evenings, but for some strange reason he felt a desire to go to this meeting. There was no doubt a conscious void within him never yet filled, and some instinctive inner voice whispered that he might find food for his soul-hunger, satisfying something he had unconsciously and blindly been groping for all his life.

That Saturday evening was the turning point in George Müller's life and destiny. He found himself in strange company, in different surroundings, and breathing a new atmosphere. His awkwardness made him feel uncertain of his welcome to the point he apologized to Brother Wagner, in whose home the meetings were held. Brother Wagner's gracious answer was: "Come as often as you please! House and heart are open to you." He didn't understand then what he learned after from blessed experience, what joy fills and thrills the hearts of praying saints when a sinner turns his feet, however timidly, toward a place of prayer!

AWARENESS OF A LIFE CHANGE BEGINS

The little group sang a hymn and then a brother who went to Africa under the London Missionary Society fell on his knees and prayed for God's blessings on the meeting. That *kneeling before God in prayer made an impression on George Müeller that began his life-change.* He was 21 years old and had never seen a man on his knees praying, and he had never knelt in prayer before God because the Prussian habit was to stand in public prayer.

The meeting continued on with a chapter read from the Word of God and because there was no ordained clergyman present, a printed sermon was read. After another hymn, Brother Wagner prayed and as he prayed George sensed a new joy springing up in his soul. On the way home he said to his friend, "All we saw on our journey to Switzerland, and all our former pleasures are nothing compared to this evening."

When he reached his room that night he does not remember if he knelt to pray, but he never forgot that a new and strange peace and rest somehow found him as he lay in his bed that night. George Müeller's eyes were half opened, as though he saw men as trees walking; but Christ had touched those eyes. He knew little of the great Healer, but somehow he had touched the hem of His garment of grace, and virtue came out of Him who wears that seamless robe, and who responds even to the faintest contact of the soul that is groping after salvation.

That Saturday evening in November, 1825, was to this young student of Halle *the parting of the ways*. He had tasted that the Lord is gracious, though he could not account for the desire for divine things. That desire made it seem too long to wait for another meal; so three times before the next Saturday he went to the house of Brother Wagner who welcomed him and helped him search the Scriptures.

Müeller's next marked step in his new path was the discovery of the preciousness of the Word of God. Of all the Scriptures he marked with great prominence was the "Little Gospel" in John 3:16, for by it he found a full salvation and his first glimpse of the plan of salvation. He found in the Word of God a great fact: the love of God in Christ, and upon that fact faith, not feeling, laid hold of him. The love of God in Christ constrained him to a love he had never experienced before and impelled and enabled him to renounce his life of sinful self-indulgence. Thus, he learned the double truth that in the blood of God's atoning Lamb is the Fountain of both forgiveness and cleansing, the sole source and secret are in Christ's work for us and in us.

The new year, 1826, was indeed a new year to this newborn soul. He now began to read missionary journals, which kindled a flame in his heart.

Chapter 2

NEW PATHWAYS AND PREPARING THE CHOSEN VESSEL ON THE POTTER'S WHEEL

FROM CONVERSION TO FULL ENTRANCE ON HIS LIFE WORK

MÜELLER was burning with the flame of the mission field in his heart and wanted to set out for that ministry immediately. However, that was not God's plan for him. God allowed George to see how unfit he was for the work he sought, his desire to teach in the mission field was impossible for he, himself, needed to be taught. Even though he was a child of God, he could not give a clear testimony or explanation of the elementary gospel truths. God held him back to prepare His chosen vessel...this is not to say that Müeller waited patiently for his training to be complete.

GOD GRACE OPENED THE SCRIPTURES TO HIM

Later, in 1826, he was asked by a schoolmaster to come and help an aged, infirm clergyman in the parish. George committed another man's sermon to memory and presented his memorized, lifeless sermon with no favorable response from the little congregation. George Müeller 'got through' his painful effort of August 27, 1826, reciting this sermon at 8 a.m. in the chapel, and three hours later in the parish church. Being asked to preach again in the afternoon, but having no second sermon committed to memory, he had to keep silent, or *depend on the Lord for help.* His conscience was not yet enlightened enough to see that he was acting a false part in preaching another man's sermon as he own. He also did not have the spiritual insight to see it is not God's way to set up a man to preach who does not know enough of either His Word or the life of the Spirit within him to prepare his own sermon. He thought he could at least read the fifth chapter of Matthew and expound on it. But he had no sooner begun the first beatitude then he felt himself greatly assisted. Not only were his lips opened, but the Scriptures opened too, his own soul expanded, and a peace and power, wholly unknown to his tame, mechanical repetitions of the morning accompanied the simple expositions of the afternoon. With this added advantage, he talked on a level with the people and not over their heads, his colloquial, earnest speech riveting their attention.

Going back to Halle, he said to himself, *"This is the true way to preach"'* even though he felt misgivings that perhaps such a simple style of exposition might not suit a cultured refined city congregation. He had yet to learn how the enticing words of man's wisdom make the Cross of Christ of none effect, and how the very simplicity that makes preaching intelligible to the illiterate makes sure that the most cultivated will also understand it, whereas the reverse is not true. Here was another very important step in his preparation for subsequent service. His first attempt at preaching taught him the need of knowing God's Word and His will the very foundation of all his future preaching. He earned the rank throughout life of being among the simplest and most scriptural preachers. He found great joy in his preaching and the harvest from it. The committed sermon of some great preacher might draw forth human praise, but it was the simple witness of the Word, and of the believer to the Word, that had praise of God.

A Change in Attitude

About this same time he took another step—perhaps the most significant thus far in its bearing on the precise form of work so closely linked with his name. For two months he availed himself of free lodgings furnished for poor divinity students in the famous Orphan Houses built by A. H. Francke, a saintly man and professor at Halle, who had died a hundred years before in 1727. Francke had established an orphanage in entire dependence upon God. The very building where this young student lodged was to him an object lesson—a visible, veritable, tangible proof that the Living God hears prayer, and can in answer to prayer alone build a house for orphan children. That lesson was never lost, and George Müeller fell into the apostolic succession of such holy labor. He often records how much his own faith work was indebted to that example of simple trust in prayer exhibited by Francke. Seven years later he read the life of Francke and was all the more prompted to follow him as he followed Christ. Half unconsciously George Müeller's whole lifework at Bristol found both its suggestion and pattern in Francke's orphanage at Halle.

At this point, we have reached another milestone in this life-journey of George Müeller, four years have gone by and it is now the end of the year 1829. God had led George on a truly remarkable pathway. In the four years, he found the straight and narrow way and began to walk in it, and now at the tender age of twenty-five he had been taught some of the powerful secrets of a holy, happy, and useful life which became the foundation of the whole structure of the rest of his life. During the four years he experience significant and eventful experiences, all of which forecast his future work. His conversion in the little primitive assembly of believers where worship and the Word of God were the only attractions was the starting point in a life for God filled with forward strides. In spite of his early life of sin it did not have the power to reproach or retard him from God's will for his life.

LEARNING RENUNCIATION AND FORSAKING WORLDLY DESIRES

Within these few years he learned advanced lessons in renunciation. Such as forsaking his desire to write novels, giving up the girl he loved, turning his back on the seductive prospect of ease and wealth, to accept self-denial for God. He severed his dependence on his father for money and also refused all salary preferring to depend on God to meet all his needs. He also chose a very simple expository form of preaching instead of catering to popular taste. Feeding on the Word of God, he cultivated habits of searching the Scriptures and praying in secret, he threw himself on God, not only for temporal needs, but for support in bearing all burdens, however great or small.

These are just a few of his experiences during those four years since his new birth that demonstrate the Hand of God molding this chosen vessel on His potter's wheel, and unmistakably shaping George Müeller for the singular service to which he was destined.

Chapter 3

PASTORAL WORK AND
MARRIAGE TO MARY GROVES

EARLY IN 1830, Müeller was preaching in a small church in Sidmouth and was approached by three sisters in the Lord asking his opinion about believers' baptism. That question became the next important step in his life. He replied that having been baptized as a child he saw no need of being baptized again. They asked him if he had prayerfully searched the Word of God on this matter and he frankly confessed he had not. With plain speech, one of the sisters replied: "I entreat you, then, never again to speak any more about it until you have done so." To which Müeller neither resented nor resisted her remark, for he was too honest and conscientious to dismiss without due reflection any challenge to search the oracles of God for their witness upon any given question. Moreover, he preached with great boldness that Christian practice must be subjected to one great test, namely, the touchstone of the Word of God.

LEARNING THE DOCTRINE OF BAPTISM

Therefore, he determined to study the subject until he could reach a final, satisfactory, and scriptural conclusion that from that time forward whether to defend infant baptism or believers' baptism, to do so only on scriptural grounds. He was humble enough to be willing to retract any erroneous teaching and renounce any false position for he truly believed in the wise maxim: "Don't be consistent, but simply be true." After much study in the Word of God and prayer he believed from the Word of God and the Spirit of God that only believers are the proper subjects of baptism and that by immersion in water, based on Act 8:36-38 and Romans 6:3-5. His conviction compelled his action, for in him there was no spirit of compromise; and he was promptly baptized.

In the same summer of 1830, the further study of the Word of God satisfied him that, though there is no direct command to do so, he would assume the scriptural and apostolic practice of breaking bread ever Lord's Day and that the Spirit of God should never be hindered in His working through any believer according to the gifts He had given them according to 1 Corinthians 12, Romans 12, and Ephesians 4, etc. These decisions brought him increasing spiritual prosperity.

ONSET OF STRONG FEELINGS REGARDING SALARY

At the same time, he began to have strong conscientious misgivings that quickly turned to convictions that he could no longer, upon the principle of obedience to the Word of God, consent to receive any stated salary as a minister of Christ. This position was based on the following grounds and became the basis of his lifelong attitude:

> ‣ Firstly, a stated salary implies a fixed sum, which cannot be paid without a fixed income through pew rentals or some such source of revenue. This practice seemed directly opposite of the teaching of the Spirit of God in James 2:1-6.

> ‣ Secondly, a fixed pew rental could very well become a burden to even a willing disciple. He felt that people would gladly contribute to a pastor's support if allowed to do so according to their own ability and convenience rather than be oppressed

the demand of a stated sum at a stated time.

▸ Thirdly, the whole system tends to become a bondage to the pastor who might be tempted to keep back or modify his message so as not to offend the main contributors toward his salary.

Therefore, satisfied with his reasons, he promptly announced his decision to receive no salary in his twenty-fifth year and for the rest of his life. Any voluntary monies given were placed in a box in the chapel over which was written that whoever had a desire to do something for his support could do so according to their desire and ability. However, to be entirely consistent he never asked help from anyone but bore the necessary costs for travel in the Lord's service, nor did he ever state his needs, he relied completely upon the Lord and Him alone. To supply all his needs and those of his family and his life work.

FINDING A WIFE

On October 7, 1830, George Müeller, in finding a wife, found a good thing and obtained new favor from the Lord. Miss Mary Groves was married to this man of God, and for forty blessed years proved to be an able helpmeet for him. It was almost, if not quite, an ideal union, for which he continually thanked God; and, although her kingdom was one which came not 'with observation,' the scepter of her influence was far wider in its sway than will ever be appreciated by those who were strangers to her personal domestic life. She was a rare woman and her price was above rubies. The heart of her husband safely trusted in her, and the great family of orphans who were to her as children rise up even to this day to call her blessed.

LIKE-MINDED IN MARRIAGE AND MINISTRY

From the very beginning of their marriage, George and

Mary's love grew, and with it, their mutual confidence and trust. One of the earliest ties that bound these two in one was the bond of self-denial, yielding literal obedience to Luke 7:33, they sold what little they had and gave alms, henceforth laying up no treasures on Earth (Matthew 6: 19-34.) Thus the step was taken—accepting for Christ's sake, voluntary poverty—was never regretted, but rather increasingly rejoiced in. They were so faithful to this step that they continued the same path of continued self-sacrifice for sixty-eight years and on to the very end of George Müeller's life. He died a poor man according to the riches of this world and when his will was admitted to probate, it showed his entire personal property to be only one hundred and sixty pounds (under $249.00 in USD).

FINAL FAREWELL TO ALL EARTHLY POSSESSIONS:

This final farewell to all earthly possessions, in 1830, left this newly married husband and wife to look only to the Lord. From that time forward they were put to ample daily testing both of their faith in the Great Provider and the faithfulness of the Great Promiser. It may not be wrong to anticipate what is yet to be more fully recorded that from that day to day, and hour to hour, during more than threescore years, George Müeller was able to set to his seal that God is true. Few men have ever been permitted to turn the smallest matters over to God's care for His children, partly because few have so completely abandoned themselves to that care. George Müeller dared to trust Him, who numbers the very hairs of our head and cares even for the sparrows, for He said, "Do not fear therefore; you are of more value than many sparrows" (Matthew 10:31). George Müeller was permitted to know as never before, and as few others have learned, how truly God may be approached as

"Thou that hearest prayer... (Psalm 65:2).

PRECIOUS PROMISES PROVEN BY 50 THOUSAND CASES

Those precious promises, which in faith and hope were "laid hold" of in 1830, were "held fast" until the end. God's divine faithfulness proved to be a safe anchor in the most prolonged and violent tempests and trials. Mr. Müeller calculated that he could trace distinct answers to prayers; and in multitudes of instances in which God's care was definitely traced like an all encompassing presence or atmosphere of life and strength.

PERSONAL LOSS BRINGS A VALUABLE LESSON LEARNED

In August of 1831, Mrs. Müeller gave birth to a stillborn baby and was seriously ill for six weeks. George lamented for a cold and carnal heart and hesitating and formal prayers even in his zeal for God. He especially chided himself for not having a more serious consideration of the peril of child-bearing, and in praying for his wife. God showed him that the prospect of parenthood for him seemed to be a new burden and hindrance in his work for the Lord. How many a servant of God has no more exalted idea of the divine privilege of a sanctified parenthood! He learned through this loss that a wife and child are most precious gifts of God when received in answer to prayer from His hands. They also help to prepare the man of God for certain parts of his work for which no other preparation is adequate. They teach valuable lessons to round out character into a far more symmetrical beauty and service. Not to forget the godly succession through many generations that holy wedlock and its fruits supply. God blessed their union and gave them more children.

SEVEN IMPORTANT EXPERIENCES THAT MOLDED MÜELLER'S MINISTRY

1. An experience of frequent and at times prolonged financial straits. Money for personal needs, and the needs for hundreds and thousands of orphans, and various branches of the work of the Scriptural Knowledge Institute was often reduced to a single *pound*, or even a *penny*, and sometimes to *nothing*. His required a constant waiting on God, and looking to Him only for all supplies. Oftentimes the supplies were furnished only from month to month, week to week, day to day, or *hour to hour!* George Müeller's faith was kept lively by perpetual training.

2. An experience of the unchanging faithfulness of the Father-God to supply. Though the times of financial straits were many, long, and trying, there was never a time when God failed to provide. "Not once, or five times, or five hundred times, but thousands of times in these threescore years have we had in hand not enough for one more meal, either in food or in funds; but not once has God failed us; not once have we or the orphans gone hungry or lacked any good thing."

3. An experience of the working of God upon the minds, hearts, and consciences of contributors to the work. Literally from the earth's ends, men, women, and children who had never seen Mr. Müeller and could have known nothing of the pressure at the time, have been led at the exact crisis of affairs to send aid in the very sum or form most needful. In countless cases, while he was on his knees asking, the answer has come so closely to the request that it shuts out all *chance* or *coincidence* as an explanation and compels belief in a prayer-hearing God.

4. An experience of habitual *hanging upon the unseen God* and nothing else. Müeller issued annual reports to the public regarding the history and progress of the work and also gave an accounting of the stewardship to the many donors. However, these reports *never made a direct appeal for aid.* At one time, Müeller withheld the annual report lest some might misconstrue the account as asking for aid. When God, the Great Provider, supplied the needed funds, Müeller sent the report out. The Living God alone was and is the Patron of these institutions; and not even the wisest and wealthiest, the noblest and the most influential of human beings, has ever been looked to as their dependence.

5. An experience of conscientious *care in accepting and using gifts.* Here is a pattern for all who are stewards of God. Whenever there was ground of misgiving as to the propriety or expediency of receiving what was offered, it was declined, however pressing the need, unless or until all such objectionable features no more existed. If the person contributing was known to dishonor lawful debts, so that the money was righteously due to others; if the gift was encumbered and held by restrictions that hindered its free use for God; it was designated for endowment purposes or a provision for Mr. Müeller's old age, or for the future of the institutions; or if there was any evidence or suspicion that the donation was given grudgingly, reluctantly, or for self-glory, it was promptly declined and returned. In some case, even when large amounts were involved, givers were urged to wait until more prayer and deliberation made clear that they were acting under diving leading.

6. An experience of divine caution lest there should be even a careless *betrayal of the fact of pressing need*, to the outside public. The helpers in the institutions were allowed to come into such close fellowship and to have such knowledge of the exact state of the work as aids not only in common labors but in common prayers and self-denials. Without such knowledge they could hot serve, pray, nor sacrifice intelligently. But they were solemnly charged that even in the most severe crisis to never reveal to anyone in the public lest the work should seem to be looking away from divine help.

7. An experience of growing boldness of faith in *asking and trusting for great things*. As faith was exercised it was energized so that it became as easy and natural to ask for a hundred, a thousand, or ten thousand pounds, as once it had been for a pound or a penny. After confidence in God had been strengthened through discipline, and God had been proven faithful, it required no more venture to cast himself on God for provision for two thousand children and an annual outlay of at least twenty-five thousand pound for them than in the earlier periods of the work to look to Him to care for twenty homeless orphans at a cost of two hundred and fifty pounds a year. Only by *using faith* are we kept from *losing it*, and to *use* faith is to *lose* the unbelief that hinders God's mighty acts.

Chapter 4

BRISTOL AND THE SEED OF GOD'S OWN PLANTING

AN INVITATION OR A CALLING?

MR. MÜELLER received a letter from Mr. Craik, a fellow minister and friend, inviting him to join him in his work at Bristol. This made such an impression on his mind that he began to prayerfully consider whether it was God's call, and if was a field white unto harvest more suitable to his calling and gifts. The following Lord's day, he was preaching on the Lord's coming, and he referred to the effect of this blessed hope in impelling God's messenger to bear witness more widely and from place to place, and reminded the brethren that he had refused to bind himself to stay with them, for at any moment he felt he needed to be free to follow the divine leading elsewhere.

ONWARD TO BRISTOL AND THE LESSON ON THE JOURNEY

On April 20, 1832, he left for Bristol. While on the journey he had no liberty to speak for Christ, or even give away tracts, and he had neglected that quiet hour with the Lord which supplies to spiritual life its breath and bread. No lesson is more important for us to learn, yet how slow we are to learn it: that for the lack of habitual seasons set apart from devout meditation upon the Word of God and for prayer, nothing else will compensate. Not conversations with Christian friends or Christian activity can be allowed to interfere with that special time of communion with our Father-God. How often we rush from one thing to another especially work for the Lord and we don't take the time to renew our strength in waiting on the Lord, as though God cared more for the *quantity* than the *quality* of our service to Him. George Müeller had the grace to detect in this lesson one of the foremost perils of a busy man in this day of almost insane hurriedness. He saw that if we are to feed others we must be fed; and that even public and united services of praise and prayer can never supply that food which is dealt out to the believer only in the closet, the place where you are shut-in and meet alone with your God.

THE SECRET OF TRUE PROSPERITY AND BLESSING

Three times in the Word of God we find a divine prescription for true prosperity. God says to Joshua, *"This book of the law shall not depart out of thy mouth; but thou shalt meditate therein day and night, that thou mayest observe to do according to all that is written therein: for then thou shalt make thy way prosperous, and the thou shalt have good success"* (Joshua 1:8).

Five hundred years later, the inspired author of Psalm 1 repeats the promise in unmistakable terms. The Spirit there says of the man whose delight is in the law of the Lord, *"But his delight is in the law of the Lord; and in His law he doth meditate day and night. And he shall be like a tree planted by the rivers of water, that bringeth forth his fruit in his season; his leaf shall not wither; and whatsoever he doeth shall prosper"* (Psalm 1:2-3).

More than a thousand years pass, and before the New Testament is sealed up as complete, once more the Spirit bears essentially the same blessed witness. *"But whoso looketh into the perfect law of liberty, and continueth therein, he being not a forgetful hearer, but a doer of the work, this man shall be blessed in his deed"* (James 1:25). The secret: true meditation, reflection on the Scriptures, (1) which are at once a book of the law, (2) a river of life, (3) and a mirror of self fitted to convey the will of God, the life of God, and the transforming power of God. The believer who for any cause neglects the prayerful study of the Word of God makes a fatal mistake. To read God's holy book, and by it search yourself, and turn it into prayer and holy living is the one great secret of growth in grace and godliness. To do God's work we much have power with God and must prevail with Him in prayer if we are to have power with men and prevail with men in any form of preaching, witnessing or serving.

SEEKING THE SECRETS OF THE LIFE OF GEORGE MÜELLER

If we seek the secrets of the life George Müeller lives and the work he did, this is the very key to the whole mystery, and with that key any believer can unlock the doors to a prosperous growth in grace and power in God's service. God's Word is His Word—the expression of His thought, the revealing of His mind and heart. The supreme end of life is to know God and make Him known; know His Word to make Him known!

MINISTRY AT GIDEON CHAPEL AND BETHESDA CHAPEL

On July 6, 1832, services were being held in both chapels with the podiums being filled by both Mr. Müeller, and Mr. Craik and both of the chapels were filled to capacity with many souls being saved.

On Preaching or Teaching the Word of God

This brought about a deeper hunger in George Müeller to give new diligence and study to the preparation of his messages to attract new souls to the Kingdom of God. In the supernatural as well as the natural there is a *law of cause and effect*.

Even the Spirit of God does not work without order and method; He has His chosen channels through which He pours blessing. There is no accident in the spiritual world. Like the wind, the Spirit bloweth where He listeth. In the armory of the Word of God are many weapons and all have their various uses and adaptations. Blessed is the workman or warrior who seeks to know what particular implement or instrument God is appointing for each particular work or conflict.

We are to study to keep in such communion with His Word and Spirit that we will be true workmen that need *"not be ashamed, rightly dividing the word of truth"* (2 Timothy 2:15). This Scripture found in Paul's second letter to Timothy is a very peculiar one. It seems to liken a true workman of the Word of God to an engineer who is given the work of constructing a direct road to a certain point. The hearer's heart and conscience is the objective and the aim of the preacher or teacher should be to use God's truth to reach the hearer's heart. He should be direct not evasive, not deceptive with apologies and arguments, but straightforward to the road of conviction and finally conversion. The preacher should study the needs of those who hear him and the best way to deal with them and then with prayer and study of the Word of God give them the gospel message to meet those needs.

GEORGE MÜELLER'S ENTRANCE INTO HIS LIFEWORK

In 1882, George read the biography of A. H. Francke, the founder of the Orphan Houses of Halle. As that life and work were undoubtedly use of God to make George Müeller a like instrument in the same kind of service and mold even the methods of philanthropy used by Mr. Francke.

August H. Francké was Müeller's fellow countryman. Around 1696, at Halle in Prussia, he had started the largest enterprise for poor children then existing in the world. He trusted God, and He whom he trusted did not fail him, but helped him throughout abundantly. His institutions resembled a large street more than a building, they were erected and housed about two thousand orphan children whom he fed, clothed, and taught the Word of God. For about thirty years all went well until God called Francké home to be with Him in 1727. After his death, his son-in-law became the director and even now after two hundred years have passed the Orphan Houses are still in existence, serving their noble purpose.

THE STRIKING RESEMBLANCE OF FRANCKE'S AND MÜELLER'S ORPHAN WORK

If you would compare the work with orphans by Francke and with that of Müeller, you would find that Müeller's work with orphans a counterpart of Francke's in many respects though Müeller started his work more than one hundred years after Francke's death. Müeller had more years at his work before God called him home; however, when Müeller died he left his work in the capable hands of his son-in-law as did Francke. Both son-in-laws have carried on the ministries through the years.

GOD'S OFTEN USES THE PATHWAY OF SUCCESS OF ONE MINISTRY TO TRAIN ANOTHER

Perhaps you have already noticed how God, when preparing a workman for a certain definite service, often leads him out of the beaten track into a path peculiarly His own by means of a powerful biography or by contact with some other living servant of God who is doing some compelling work for God and exhibiting the spirit that must guide if there is to be true success. Meditation on Francke's life and work naturally led Müeller, who way hungering for a wider usefulness, to think more of the poor homeless children around him and to ask whether he also, with God's help could make some way to provide for them; and as he was meditating and musing on this the spark that lit the fire began to burn in him.

FIRST STEPS TO ORPHAN MINISTRY

In June of 1833, when he was almost twenty-eight years old, the inward flame began to take shape in a way to help the orphans which proved to be the first step toward his lifelong work with them. It occurred to him to go out on the streets around eight o'clock each morning and gather the poor children and give them bread for their breakfast. Then for about an hour or so he began to teach them from the Bible and also he began to teach them to also read. Later on in the morning he also did the same for the adults and aged poor. He began at once to feed from thirty to forty persons, confident that, as the number increased, the Lord's provision would increase also.

When he told his friend and associate, Mr. Craik what he was doing, Mr. Craik guided him to a place that would hold one hundred and fifty children that could be rented for ten shillings a year and also led him to an aged brother who would gladly undertake the teaching of the children. Obstacles unexpectedly prevented the plan to come to fruition, however, it only served to plant the seed deeper in Müeller and center his thoughts and aims in the direction of caring for orphans.

In 1834, prior to the orphanage work, God laid on the heart of George Müeller to found "The Scriptural Knowledge Institution for Home and Abroad," this was an outreach ministry of his life work that no doubt had part in laying the strong foundation of his faith in the provision of God alone especially for the Orphanage Ministry. He and Mr. Craik confidently believed that the work of the Lord could be best served within the landmarks and limits set up in His Word and thus doing so would give boldness in prayer and confidence in labor. They desired the work itself to be a witness to the living God, and a testimony to believers, by calling attention to the objectionable methods already in us and encouraging all God's true servants in adhering to the principles and practices which He has sanctioned.

OBJECTS OF THE INSTITUTION

- To establish or aid day-schools, Sunday-schools, and adult-schools, taught and conducted only by believers and on thoroughly scriptural principles.
- To circulate the Holy Scriptures, wholly or in portions, over the widest territory.
- To aid missionary efforts and assist laborers in the Lord's vineyard anywhere who were working upon a biblical basis and looking to the Lord for support.
- Every believer's duty and privilege is to help on the cause and work of Christ.

- The patronage of the world is not to be sought after, depended upon, or countenanced.

- Pecuniary (financial) aid, or help in managing or carrying on its affairs is not to be asked for or sought from those who are not believers.

- Debts are not to be contracted or allowed for any cause in the work of the Lord.

- The standard of success is not to be a numerical or financial standard.

- All compromise of the truth or any measures that impair testimony to God are to be avoided. Thus the Word of God was accepted as counselor, and all dependence was on God's blessing in answer to prayer.

ONE SHILLING LEFT

Mr. Müeller noted this sentence in his journal at the time the plans and purpose for the Institution were drawn up. "We have only one shilling left." Surely no advance step would have been taken, had not the eyes been turned, not on the empty purse, but on the full and exhaustless treasury of a rich and bountiful Lord! It was plainly God's purpose that, out of such abundance of poverty, the riches of His liberality should be manifested. It pleased Him; from whom and by whom are all things, that the work should be begun when His servants were poorest and weakest so that its growth to such giant proportions might prove to be a plant of His own right hand's planting, and that His Word might be fulfilled in its whole history.

"I the Lord do keep it; I will water it every moment:
Lest any hurt it, I will keep it night and day."
(Isaiah 27:3)

The Scriptural Knowledge Institution for Home and

Abroad opened its doors in March of 1834 to the glory of God. Immediately the work became established and by October there were one hundred and twenty children in the Sunday school, forty in the adult classes, there were two hundred and nine boys and girls in the four day-schools. Four hundred and eighty-two Bibles and five hundred and twenty Testaments had been put in circulation, and fifty-seven pounds had been spent in aid of missionary operations. During these seven months the Lord had sent in answer to prayer over one hundred and sixty seven pounds of money and much blessing upon the work itself. The brothers and sisters who were in charge had been given by the same prayer answering God in direct response to the cry of need and the supplication of faith.

THE ORPHANS

Meanwhile *another object* was coming into even greater prominence in the mind and heart of George Müeller...*the thought of making permanent provision for fatherless and motherless children.* An orphan boy who had been in the school had been taken to the poorhouse. This incident set Mr. Müeller praying for the timing of the seed God had planted in his soul, the seed had taken root and was springing up and growing, he knew not how. As yet it was only in the blade, but in time there would come the ear and the full-grown corn in the ear, the new seed of a larger harvest.

THE WORK OF THE POTTER EXAMINED

The steps in the process God used to shape His vessel for His purpose, educating and preparing George Müeller for His work:

1. His conversion: in a most unforeseen manner and unexpected time.

2. His missionary spirit: that consuming flame kindled and caused willingness for whatever God required.

3. His renunciation of self: God enabled him to give up many earthly attachments and vices.

4. His taking counsel of God: he formed the habit early in things great and small to seek God's will in all things.

5. His humble and childlike faith: the Father drew him to Himself and taught him to submit to his fatherly counsel and guidance.

6. His method of preaching: he preached in total dependence on the Spirit of God to expound on the Scriptures.

7. His cutting loose from man: step by step all dependence on man for financial aid in any form was abandoned: he turned to God alone as his Provider.

8. His satisfaction in the Word: his knowledge of Scriptures grew as did his love for the divine oracles increased. He fixed the teachings in the Bible in his mind by meditation and practice.

9. His thorough Bible study: he systematically searched the Scriptures for the treasures of God's truth.

10. His freedom from human control: he felt the need of independence of man in order to have complete dependence on God.

11. His use of opportunity: he felt the value of souls and formed habits of approaching others as to the matters of salvation even in public conveyances. He witnessed by word, tract, and humble example and sought constantly to lead someone to Christ.

12. His companions in service: his most efficient co-workers Brother Craik, and his wife, Mary, both

of them proving to be God's gift to the ministry and great aids in bearing burdens of responsibility.

13. His waiting on God for a message: in every occasion he asked God for a word in season, then a mode of treatment, and unction in delivering it in godly simplicity and sincerity with the demonstration of the Spirit.

14. His submission to authority of the Word: he submitted himself to the practices of the Scripture and walked according to any new light God gave him.

15. His stress upon voluntary offerings: he taught that all work of God should be maintained by the freewill gifts of believers.

16. His surrender of all earthly possessions: he and his wife literally sold all their possessions and gave alms, henceforth to live by the day.

17. His habit of secret prayer: he learned early to prize communion with God and regarded it as his highest duty and privilege.

18. His love of orphans: his loving heart had been drawn out toward poverty and misery everywhere, but especially in the case of destitute children with no parents.

19. In addition to these steps of preparation he knew that God had guided him from the time of his birth, through to his ministry and thus the chosen vessel, shaped for its great use, had by the same divine Hand been brought to the very place where God planted him for his life of service to God by building orphanages by God's total provision. He saw and felt that he was only an earthen vessel that God had both chosen and filled him for the work he was to do and while this conviction made him happy in his

work, it made him humble too. The older he grew the more humble he became. He felt more and more his utter insufficiency and it grieved him that human eyes would ever turn away from the Potter to the clay, and he perpetually sought to avert their gaze from himself to God alone. *"For of him, and through him, and to him, are all things: to whom be glory for ever. Amen"* (Romans 11:36).

Chapter 5

GROWTH IN GOD'S WORD,
PRAYER AND LEADING

THESE were the last great and preliminary steps before George Müeller entered into his lifelong ministry of founding orphanages to the glory of God.

THE MOST IMPORTANT STEP

Nothing is more worthy of imitation, perhaps, than the uniformly deliberate, self-searching, and prayerful way in which he set about this massive undertaking. It was preeminently so in attempting this new form of service, the future growth of which was not then even in his thoughts. In daily prayer he sought the Master's presence to sift from the pure grain of a godly purpose to glorify Him, all the chaff of selfish and carnal motives, to get rid of every taint of worldly self-seeking or lust of applause, and to bring every thought into captivity to the Lord. He constantly probed his heart to discover the secret and subtle impulses that are unworthy of a true servant of God; and believing that a spiritually minded brother often helps one to an insight into his own heart, he spoke often to Brother Craik about his plans, praying God to use him as a means of exposing any unworthy motive, or of suggesting any scriptural objections to his project. His honest aim was to please God, he yearned to know his own heart, and welcomed any light that revealed his real self and prevented a mistake. Mr. Craik very decidedly encouraged him, and further prayer so confirmed previous impressions of God's guidance that on December 2, 1835, the first formal step was taken in ordering printed announcements of a public meeting for the following week. The announcement stated the proposal to open an orphan house was to be laid before the brethren and further light was to be sought from them as they united in prayer with him for the mind of the Lord.

Three days later, in reading the Psalms, he was struck with these nine words: *"Open thy mouth wide, and I will fill it"* (Psalm 81:10). From that moment this text formed one of his great life mottos, and this promise became a power in molding all his work. Up to that time he had not prayed for the supply of money or helpers but now he was led to pray this Scripture confidently for his orphanage plan. He boldly asked at once for premises, and for a thousand pounds, and for suitable helpers to take charge of the children. Two days after his prayer he received the first gift of money, one shilling, and within two days more the first donation in furniture, a large wardrobe.

PUBLIC MEETING DAY

December 9th, the day for the memorable public meeting finally arrived, the preceding days had been filled with the enemy's fiery darts and Müeller was tired and low in spirit. The enemy had been whispering in his ear , and he didn't need any help from him because in his mind he had thoughts of the possibility he was going in the wrong direction as he thought of how this step if he were wrong could cause him humiliation, and more importantly reproach to his Master. Lo and behold, as soon as he reached the podium and opened his mouth to speak, help was given to him. He was borne up in the Everlasting Arms and had the full assurance that the work was of the Lord. He commenced to tell those in the meeting 3 chief reasons for establishing an orphan home:

1. That God may be glorified in so furnishing the means as to show that it is not a vain thing to trust in Him.

2. That the spiritual welfare of fatherless and motherless children may be promoted.

3. That their temporal good may be secured.

It was proposed to take in only those children that had no parents at the age from seven to twelve, thought later on younger orphans were also admitted. The boys were brought up to work in a trade and the girls for service (maids, nannies, etc.) and all of them were to have a plain education to meet the needs of their lifework.

GOD'S FAITHFUL PROVISION

As soon as the enterprise was launched, the Lord's power and will to provide began at once and increasingly to appear. Therefore, from this point on George Müeller's daily journal and journey of faith is one long record of man's faith and supplication and God's faithfulness and guidance.

A foremost need was that of able and suitable helpers, which only God could supply. Mr. Müeller felt he must have men and women who were likeminded, and would naturally care for the state of the orphans and of the work. Before he prayed, the Lord answered. As early as December 10th a brother and sister had willingly offered themselves, and the spirit that moved them shows in the language of the letter below:

"We propose ourselves for the service of the intended orphan house, if you think us qualified for it; also to give up all the furniture which the Lord has given us for the use of the orphanage, and to do this without receiving any salary whatever; believing that if it be the will of the Lord to employ us, He will supply all our need." Other self-giving proposals followed proving that God's people are willing to be used of Him in the day of His power. He who wrought in His servant to will and to work sent helpers to share his burdens and to this day has met all similar needs out of His riches in glory. There has never been any lack of competent, cheerful, and devoted helpers though the work expanded rapidly and for an extended time.

AN IMPORTANT OMISSION

Though Müeller had brought all his needs before the Lord and asked for faith in building, furnishing, rent money and other expenses the confesses *he had never once asked the Lord to send the orphans!* The appointed day came for receiving applications to receive orphans and *not one application* was made. Everything was ready *except the orphans.* All that evening he literally lay on his face before God and felt so low that he told God if it would glorify Him more he would be willing to rejoice in the fact that all the plans for the orphanage would come to nothing. However, that was not God's plan, the very next day the first application was made for admission and on succeeding days from April 11th to May 18th, twenty-six orphans were in the house and more expected daily. The first house had scarcely been opened for girls when the way for the second was made plain, suitable premises were obtained on the same street and a well-fitted matron was given in answer to prayer to care for them. By April there were thirty orphans in each house. As the orphans flowed in and the need for more buildings, food, clothes, helpers, etc. increased. Müeller shared an important point regarding prayer for God to supply. As founder of this orphan work who at first asked for one thousand pounds from God, he tells us that in his own mind the thing was *as good as done*, so that he often gave thanks for large sums as though already in hand. *"Therefore I say unto you, What things soever ye desire, when ye pray, believe that ye receive them, and ye shall have them"* (Mark 11:24). This habit of counting a promise fulfilled had much to do with the triumphs of his faith and the success of his labor. He had need to another thousand pounds and he felt that God would be honored if the monies were received from the Lord, *without anyone having been asked to contribute,* before he published his Narrative *(His daily journal that proved a great blessing to many, being widely read and remarkably used to convert sinners and quicken saints.)* Therefore, he set to praying and on June 15th the whole sum was complete with no appeal made but to the Living God before whom he had brought his petition daily for eighteen months and ten days!

AN EXAMPLE OF GIVING

Among the first givers was a poor seamstress who brought the surprising sum of one hundred pounds, this singular self-denial and whole hearted giving exhibited making this a peculiarly sacred offering and a token of God's favor. There was a significance in His choice of a poor, sickly, seamstress as His instrument for laying the foundation for this great work. He who works all thing after the counsel of His own will, passing by the rich, mighty, and noble of this world chose again the poor, weak, base, despised nothings, that no flesh would glory in His presence.

A NEED FOR GROWTH IN GRACE

In 1837, George Müeller had been thirty-two years in ministry to the orphans and he began to feel a deep conviction that to his own growth in grace, godliness, and power for service two things were quite indispensable: first, more time for secret communion with God, even at the expense of his public work; and second more of a provision for the spiritual oversight of the flock of God in *Bethesda & Gideon Chapels* the total number now nearing four hundred plus the work in *The Scriptural Knowledge Institute for Home and Abroad.*

His outward work was too constant for inward reflection, and he saw that there was a risk of losing peace and power, and that activity in the most sacred sphere must not be so absorbing as to prevent holy meditation on the Word of God and fervent supplication. The Lord said first to Elijah, *"Go hide thyself"*; then, *'Go, show thyself."* He who does not first hide himself in the secret place to be alone with God is unfit to show himself in the public place to move among men. Mr. Müeller afterward used to say to brethren who had "too much to do" to spend proper time with God that four hours of work for which one hour of prayer prepares is better than five hours of work with the praying left out for our service to our Master is more acceptable and our mission to man profitable, when it is saturated with the moisture of God's blessing—the dew of the Holy Spirit. Whatever is gained in quantity is lost in quality when one engagement follows another without proper intervals for refreshment and renewal of strength by waiting on God. No man, perhaps since John Wesley has accomplished so much even in as long a life as George Müeller; yet few have ever withdrawn so often or so long into the prayer closet. In fact, from one point of view his life seems more given to supplication and intercession than to mere action of occupation among men.

GODS PROVISION

At the same time, he felt that the care of souls must not be neglected due to his absorption in either prayer or work for both believers and those seeking salvation needed pastoral oversight. Neither he nor Brother Craik had time enough for visiting so large a flock scattered over the city; and about fifty new members were added each year that had special need of teaching and care. Because there were two separate congregations the number of meetings was almost doubled; greeting and care for visitors from near and far, the endless correspondence and the oversight of the Lord's work generally consumed so much time that even with two pastors the needs of the church could not be met. At a meeting of both congregations these matters were frankly discussed with the believers and it was made plain that other helpers needed to be provided and the two churches were to be united as one to lessen the number of meetings.

OBEDIENCE TO SCRIPTURE BROUGHT A THIRD ORPHAN HOUSE

In October, 1837, a building was secured for a third orphan house for boys; but the neighbors strongly opposed its use as a charitable institution. Mr. Müeller, with meekness of spirit at once relinquished all claim upon the premises being mindful of the Scripture, *"If it be possible, as much as lieth in you, live peaceably with all men"* (Romans 12:18). He felt sure that the Lord would provide and his faith rewarded in the speedy supply of a building on the same street where the other two orphan homes were.

Chapter 6

THE WORD OF GOD AND PRAYER

ABIT both shows and makes the man, for it is at once historic and prophetic, the mirror of the man as he is and the mold of the man as he is to be. At this point, therefore, let's look at two marked habits of the man we are studying.

THREE BIOGRAPHIES THAT INFLUENCED GEORGE MÜELLER'S LIFE AND MINISTRY

Early in the year 1838, along with the biographies of Francké and John Newton who had such a singular influence on his own life, he began reading the *Life of George Whitefield*. The life story of the orphans friend had given the primary impulse to this work; the life story of a converted blasphemer had suggested his narrative of the Lord's dealings and now the life story of the great evangelist was blessed of God to shape his general character and give new power to his preaching and his wider ministry to souls. These three biographies together probably affected the whole inward and outward life of George Müeller more than any other volumes except the Word of God, and they were wisely fitted of God to co-work toward such a blessed result. The example of Francké incited to faith in prayer and to a work whose sole dependence was on God, Newton's witness to grace led to a testimony to the same sovereign love and mercy as seen in his own case. Whitefield's experience inspired to greater fidelity and earnestness in preaching the Word of God and to greater confidence in the anointing power of the Holy Spirit.

A PARTICULAR IMPRESSION DEEPLY MADE ON GEORGE MÜELLER'S MIND AND HEART

George Whitefield's unparalleled success in evangelistic labor was plainly traceable to two causes and could not be separated from them as direct effects; namely, his unusual prayerfulness, and his habit of reading the Bible on his knees. The great evangelist had learned the first lesson in service, his utter nothingness and helplessness that he was nothing, and could do nothing without God. He could neither understand the Word of God for himself, nor apply it to his own life or the life of others with power, unless the Holy Spirit became to him both insight and unction. Hence his success; he was filled with the Spirit: and this alone accounts for both the quality and the quantity of his labors. He died in 1770, at the age of fifty-six. He preached his first sermon in Gloucester in 1736 and for thirty-four years he labored unceasingly bringing the Word of God wherever God sent him. At one point in America, he preached one hundred and seventy-five times in seventy-five days, besides traveling in the slow vehicles of those days over eight hundred miles. When his health declined he was told he could only preach one sermon each week day and three on Sunday. His anointed preaching drew and held half-breathless more than thirty thousand hearers on Boston Common and made tears pour down the sooty faces of colliers (coal miners) at Kingswood, England.

The passion of George Müeller's soul was to fully know the secrets of prevailing with God and with man. George Whitefield's life drove home the truth that God alone could create in him a holy earnestness to win souls and qualify him for such divine work by imparting a compassion for the lost that would become an absorbing passion for their salvation. And, let this be carefully marked as another secret of this life of service, *Müeller himself began to read the Word of God upon his knees and often found hours great blessing in such meditation and prayer over a single psalm or chapter.*

These habits naturally lead to self-searching and comparison of the actual life with the example and pattern shown in the Word. The precept compels the practice to be seen in the light of its teaching; the command challenges the conduct to appear for examination. The prayer, whether spoken or unspoken, will inevitably be:

"Search me, O God, and know my heart,
Try me, and know my thoughts;
And see if there be any wicked way in me,
And lead me in the way everlasting."
(Psalm 139:23-24.)

THESE WORDS REVERENTLY READ WILL TRANSLATE INTO THE LIFE AND MOLD THE CHARACTER INTO THE IMAGE OF GOD.

"But we all, with open face beholding as in a glass the glory of the Lord, are changed into the same image from glory to glory, even as by the Spirit of the Lord" (2 Corinthians 3:18). But perhaps the greatest advantage will be that the Holy Scriptures will thus suggest the very words that become the dialect of prayer. *"We know not what we should pray for as we ought"* (Romans 8:26). For here is the Holy Spirit's own inspired utterance and if the praying is the example of His teaching how can we go astray? Here is our God-given liturgy and litany, a divine prayer book. We have God's promises, precepts, warning, and counsels, not to forget to mention all of the Spirit-inspired prayers. If we reflect on these prayers our own prayers will be cast in a mold that will turn precept and promise,

warning and counsel into supplication with the assurance that we cannot be asking anything that is not according to His will, for are we not turning His own Word into prayer? George Müeller found it to be and in meditating on Hebrews 13:8: *"Jesus Christ the same yesterday, and to day, and for ever.* Translating it into prayer, he sought God with the confidence that the prayer was already granted, and the need supplied and the assurance was also given that the same unchangeable love and power would continue to provide. Therefore, a promise was not only turned into prayer, but into prophecy and assurance of blessing and a river of joy at once poured into and flowed through George Müeller's soul.

AN OFTEN ASKED QUESTION

In reply to an often asked question from people who could not understand the secret of his peace, or how any many who had so many children to clothes and feed could carry such prostrating loads of care, he had one reply only: "By the grace of God, this is no cause of anxiety to me. These children I have years ago cast upon the Lord. The whole work is His, and it becomes me to be without carefulness. In whatever points I am lacking, in this point I am able by grace of God to roll the burden upon my heavenly Father."

And as the demands of the work came more and more heavily upon him. He cast the loads he could not carry upon Him who, before George Müeller was born, was the Father of the fatherless.

TEMPTED TO LAY FUNDS ASIDE
FOR FUTURE NEED

A trial of faith confronted Müeller in July of 1838 when in over a twelve month period there were in hand seven hundred and eighty pounds; that sum was reduced to twenty pounds. Mr. & Mrs. Mueller, Mr. Craik, and one other brother connected with the Boy's Orphan House, were the only four persons permitted to know of the low state of funds, after which they gave themselves to prayer. And let it be observed that Mr. Müeller testifies that his own faith was kept even stronger than when the larger sum was on hand a year before; and this faith was no mere fancy, for, although the supply was so low and shortly thirty pounds would be needed, notice was given for seven more children to enter, and it was further proposed to announce readiness to receive five others. The trial hour had come, but was not past. Less than two months later the money supply ran so low that it was needful that the Lord give by day and almost by hour if the needs were to be met. In answer to prayer for help God seemed to say, "Mine hour is not yet come." Many pounds would shortly be required toward which there was not one penny in hand. Then one day over four pounds came in, the thought occurred to Mr. Müeller, *"Why not lay aside three pounds against the coming need?"* But immediately he remembered that it is written: *"Take therefore no thought for the morrow: for the morrow shall take thought for the things of itself. Sufficient unto the day is the evil thereof"* (Matthew 6:34). He unhesitatingly cast himself upon God and paid out the whole amount for salaries then due, leaving himself again penniless.

BROTHER CRAIK'S TIMELY SERMON

At this time, Brother Craik was led to preach a sermon on Abraham, from Genesis 11, making prominent two facts: first, that so long as he acted in faith and walked in the will of God, all went well; but that second, so far as he distrusted the Lord and disobeyed Him, all ended in failure. Mr. Müeller heard this sermon and conscientiously applied it to himself. He drew two very practical conclusions that he had abundant opportunity to put into practice:

1. First, he must go into no byways or paths of his own for deliverance out of a crisis.

2. That in proportion as he had been permitted to honor God and bring some glory to His name by trusting Him, he was in danger of dishonoring Him.

The Lord immediately tested him as to how far he would venture upon them. While in such sore need of money for the orphan work, he had in the bank some two hundred and twenty pounds entrusted to him for other purposes. He might use this money for the time at least, and so relieve the present distress. The temptation to do so was strong because he knew the donors and knew them to be liberal supporters of the orphans; and he had only to explain to them the straits he was in and they would gladly consent to any appropriation of their gift that he might see best. Most men would have cut the Gordian Knot (a legendary knot tied by King Gordius of Phrygia and cut by Alexander the Great with his sword after hearing an oracle promise that whoever could undo it would be the next ruler of Asia) without hesitation. Not so for George Müeller, he saw at once that this would *be finding a way of his own out of difficulty instead of waiting on the Lord for deliverance. Moreover, he also saw that it would be forming a habit of trusting to such expedients of his own, which in other trials would lead to a similar course and hinder the growth of faith.* I used italics above because this is one of the tests by which this man of faith was proven; and we see how he kept consistently and persistently to the one great purpose of his life—to demonstrate to all men that *to rest solely on the promise of a faithful God* is the only way to know for one's self and prove to others, His faithfulness.

GEORGE MÜELLER SHARES HIS WAY OF PRAYER TAUGHT BY THE SCRIPTURES

At his times of dire need, this man who had determined to risk everything upon God's Word of promise turned from doubtful devices and questionable methods of prayer to *pleading with God*. At this point it would be wise to share his manner of pleading. He used holy argument in prayer. He goes on to explain this method of holy argument meaning putting our cause before God as an advocate would plead before a judge. To some it almost seems like a lost art but to many it actually seems childish. However, it is abundantly taught in the Scriptures. Abraham in his plea for Sodom (Genesis 18:22) is the first great example of it. Moses excelled in this art, in many crises interceding in behalf of the people revealing supreme mastery of skill. Elijah on Mount Carmel is a striking example of power in this special pleading. What holy zeal and jealousy for God! It is probable that if we had fuller records we would find that all pleaders with God, like Noah, Job, Samuel, David, Daniel, Jeremiah, Paul, and James have used the same method.

Of course God does not need to be convinced: no arguments can make any plainer to Him the claims of trusting souls to His intervention, claims based upon His own Word and confirmed by His oath. And yet, He will be inquired of and argued with. That is His way of blessing. He loves to have us set before Him our cause and His own promises: He delights in the well ordered plea where argument is piled upon argument. See how the Lord Jesus Christ commended the persistent argument of the woman of Canaan who with the wit of importunity actually turned His own objection into reason. He said in

Matthew 15:26-28, *"It is not meet to take the children's bread and cast it to the little dogs."* *"Truth, Lord,"* she answered, *"yet the little dogs under the master's tables eat of the crumbs which fall from the children's mouths!"* What a triumph of argument! Catching the Master himself in His Words, as He meant she should, and turning His apparent reason for not granting into a reason for granting her request. "O woman," said He, "great is thy faith! Be it unto thee even as thou wilt"—thus, as Martin Luther said, "flinging the reins on her neck."

This case stands distinctive in the Word of God, and it is this use of argument in prayer that makes it solitary in grandeur. There is another case that is parallel, that of the centurion of Capernaum, who, when our Lord promised to go and heal his servant, argued that such coming was not needful since He had only to speak the healing word. Notice the basis of his argument: if he, a commander exercising authority and yielding himself to higher authority, both obeyed the word of his superior and exacted obedience from his subordinate, how much more could the Great Healer, in His absence, by a word of command wield the healing power that in His presence was obedient to His will! The Lord said: "I have no found so great faith, no, not in Israel!" (See Matthew 8:5-10.)

We are to argue our case with God, obviously not to convince Him, but to convince *ourselves*. In proving to Him that by His own word and oath and character, He has bound himself to intervene, and we demonstrate to our own faith that He has given us the right to ask and claim, and that He will answer our plea because He cannot deny himself. Therefore, we have not only examples of holy argument in prayer, but concessions of the living God himself, that when we have His Word to plead we may claim the fulfillment of His promise, not only on the ground of mercy, but of

His truth, faithfulness, and justice. Hence the holy boldness with which we are bidden to present our plea at the throne of grace. God owes to His faithfulness to do what He has promised, and to His justice not to exact a penalty from the sinner, a penalty already borne in the sinner's behalf by His own Son.

Perhaps no man of his generation has sought God after this manner of holy argument more than George Müeller. He was one of the elect few to whom it has been given to revive and restore this lost art of pleading with God. *What a period of rebirth of faith would come to the Church if all believers would learn this blessed lesson of holy argument!*

George Müeller learned well the promises of God, as he came upon a promise such as an authorized declaration of God concerning himself, names and titles He had chosen to express and reveal His true nature and will, injunctions and invitations that gave the believer a right to pray with boldness and supplication. When he saw all these fortified and exemplified by the instances of prevailing prayer, he laid these arguments up in his memory and then on occasions of great need brought them out and spread them before a prayer hearing God. It is beautiful to follow this humble man of God into the secret place and find him pouring out his soul in these argumentative pleadings as though He must convince Him to interpose to save His own name and Word from dishonor.

An Example of His Praying to God using Holy Argument

These are your orphans, for did you not declare yourself the Father of the fatherless? This is your work, for did you not call your servant to do your bidding, and what is that servant but an instrument that could neither fit itself nor use itself? Can the rod lift itself, or the saw move itself, or the hammer deal its own blow and the sword make its own thrust? And if this is your work, are you not bound to care for your own work? And was not all this deliberately planned and carried out for your own glory? And would you suffer your own glory to be dimmed? Were not your own Words given and confirmed by your oath and could you allow your promise, thus sworn to, to be dishonored even in the least bit? Are not the half-believing Church and the unbelieving world watching to see how you, the Living God, will stand by your own unchanging assurance, and would you supply an argument for the skeptic and the scoffer? Would you not, must you not, rather put new proofs of your faithfulness in the mouth of your saints and furnish increasing arguments to silence the caviling tongue and put to shame the hesitating believer?

This is how the lowly-minded saint in Bristol, George Müeller, pleaded with God for more than sixty years, and God honored his faith, perseverance, obedience and selfless desire to feed, clothe, and bring up in the admonition of the Lord, thousands of orphaned boys and girls to the glory of God, the Father to the fatherless.

Chapter 7

TRIALS OF FAITH AND HELPERS TO FAITH

GOD has His own mathematics: we need only witness the miracle of the loaves and fishes. Our Lord said to the disciples: "Give ye them to eat," and as they divided, He multiplied the scanty provision; as they subtracted from it He added to it; as they decreased it by distributing, He increased it. (See Luke 9:10.)

ADDING HELPERS

It has been beautifully said of all holy partnerships, that griefs shared are divided, and joys shared are multiplied. At first when the work began George Müeller had God alone for his partner, and later on, several more were added including Mrs. Müeller, Mr. Craik, and one or two helpers were permitted to know the condition of the funds and supplies. Later still in the autumn of 1838, he began to feel that he ought to more fully bring into confidence others who shared in the toils of caring for the orphans by having them join in prayers and therefore in the knowledge of the needs that prayer was to supply; or else how could they fully be partakers of the faith, the work, and the reward? Not only that, how could they feel the full proof of the presence of God in the answers to prayer, know the joy of the Lord which such answers inspire, or praise Him for the deliverance that such answers bring about. It seemed plain that they must know the depths of need, the extremities of want out of which God had lifted them and then ascribe the glory, honor and praise to His name.

Therefore, Mr. Müeller called together all the beloved brothers and sisters linked with him in the conduct of the work and fully stated the case keeping nothing back. He showed them the distress they were in, but told them to be of good courage, assuring them of his own confidence that help was near at hand. He then invited them to join with him and the few others in the prayer circle in supplication to Jehovah Jireh.

This step was of no small importance to all concerned, for a considerable number of praying believers were added to the band of intercessors that gave God no rest day or night with their prayers. Mr. Müeller also laid down the principles the work was founded on reminding all concerned that nothing must be bought, whatever the need, for which there was not money in hand to pay, and yet it must be equally a settled principle that the children must not be lacking anything needful; for better that the work cease and the orphans sent away rather than have them kept in a home to suffer hunger or nakedness. Again, nothing was ever to be revealed to outsiders of any existing need, lest it be construed into an appeal for help, for the only resort must be the living God. He often reminded the helpers that the supreme object of the institutions founded in Bristol was to prove God's faithfulness and the perfect safety of trusting solely to His promises. Pleasing Him, therefore, meant to restrain all tendency to look to man for help. They were also encouraged to seek daily fellowship and communion with the Lord to grow in their faith and trust in God and help in their supplications for the children. They were warned that even one discordant note may prevent the harmonious symphony of united prayer thereby hindering the acceptableness of such prayer with God.

Thus informed and instructed these devoted coworkers with the beloved founder of the orphan work met the crises intelligently. In 1840, the circle of prayer was further enlarged by admitting to its intimacies of fellowship and supplication the brothers and sisters who labored in the day schools with the same solemn injunctions repeated to them of God only knowing the needs. This proved to be an even greater blessing and especially to the helpers themselves as the earnest, believing, importunate prayers were multiplied by the increased number of believers.

KNOWLEDGE AND BLESSING FOR THE HELPERS

One very important blessing, in an inspiring sense, was the knowledge imparted to each of the helpers that this desperately needed work of housing, feeding, teaching, caring and praying for hundreds on up to thousands of orphans was not George Müeller's work only, but also theirs. They also sacrificed of their substance by giving cherished treasures such as jewels, ornaments and oftentimes the "widow's two mites." Their giving was like the alabaster flask of ointment which was broken upon the feet of Jesus as a willing sacrifice. They gave all they could spare and often what they could ill spare, so that there might be meat in God's house and no lack of bread or other needed supplies for His little ones. It was in thus giving that all these helpers found a new power, assurance, and blessing in praying; for as one of them said, he felt it would scarcely be *upright to pray, except he were to give what he had.*

QUESTION ASKED BY A GROUP OF VISITORS

A gentleman and some ladies visiting the orphan houses saw the large number of little ones to be cared for. One of the ladies said to the matron of the Boy's House: "Of course you cannot carry on these institutions without a good stock of funds" and the gentleman added, "Have you a good stock?" The quiet answer was, *"Our funds are deposited in a bank which cannot break." The reply drew tears from the eyes of the lady, and a gift of five pounds from the pocket of the gentleman*—a donation most opportune as there was *not one penny then in hand.*

His helpers, fellow laborers with him, who asked nothing for themselves, but cheerfully looked to the Lord for their own supplies, and willingly parted with their own money or goods in the hours of need filled Mr. Müeller's heart with praise to God, and held up his hands as Aaron and Hur sustained those of Moses, till the sun of his life went down. During all the years of his work with the orphanages these were the main human support of his faith and courage. They met with him in daily prayer, faithfully kept the secrets of the Lord's work in the great trials of faith, and when the hour of triumph came they felt it to be both duty and privilege to give testimony in the Annual Report of the gifts they were enabled to supply to the glory and praise of God.

An interesting and blessed note: George Müeller prayed in thousands of pounds during his lifetime for the needs of the orphanages, the Institute, and missionary needs etc, and at the end of his life, were you to pick up, shake and look inside George Müeller's little black coin purse, you would find all he had to his name: a few coins that jingled when you shook the purse...nothing else.

George Müeller reversed the role of giving by reserving only the most frugal sum for personal needs so that the entire remainder might be given to those in need. Mr. Müeller's own words were:

> "My aim never was how much I could obtain,
> but rather how much I could give."

To one who asked him the secret of his service he said, *"There was a day when I died, utterly died;"*

and as he spoke, he bent lower and lower,
until he almost touched the floor

— *"died to George Müeller, his opinions,
preferences, tastes and will*

— *died to the world, its approval or censure*

— *died to the approval or blame even of my
brethren and friends*

— *and since then I have studied only to show myself
approved unto God."*

Chapter 8

THE SHADOW OF A GREAT SORROW

"WITH *clouds He covereth the light*" (Job 36:32). No human life is without some experience of clouded skies and stormy days, and sometimes "*the clouds return after the rain*" (Psalm 147:8). It is a blessed experience to recognize the silver lining on the darkest storm cloud, and better still to be sure the shining of God's light behind a sky that seems wholly and hopelessly overcast.

The year 1870 was made forever pathetically memorable by the death of Mrs. Müeller, who lived just long enough to see the last of the New Orphan Houses opened. From the outset of the work in November, 1835, for more than thirty-four years, this beloved, devoted wife had been a sympathetic helper.

This wedded life had approached very near to the ideal of connubial bliss, by reason of mutual fitness, common faith in God and love for His work, and long association in prayer and service. In their case, the days of courtship were never passed; indeed the tender and delicate mutual attentions of those early days rather increased than decreased as the years went on; and the great maxim was both proven and illustrated, that the secret of willing love is the secret of keeping it. Moreover, such affection grows and becomes more and more a fountain of mutual delight. Never had his beloved "Mary" been so precious to her husband as during the very year of her departure.

This marriage union was so happy that Mr. Müeller could not withhold his loving witness that he never saw her at any time after she became his wife, without a new feeling of delight. And day by day they looked forward to finding at least a few moments of rest together, sitting after dinner, hand in hand, in loving conversation of mind and heart. Made the more complete by this touch of physical contact, and, whether in speech or silence, communing in the Lord. Their happiness in God and in each other was perennial, perpetual, and growing as the years fled by.

Mr. Müeller's solemn conviction was that all this wedded bliss was due to the fact that she was not only a devoted Christian, but that their one united object was to live only and wholly for God. That they had always abundance of work for God, in which they were heartily united. That this work was never allowed to interfere with the care of their own souls, or their seasons of private prayer and study of the Scriptures. Finally, that they secured a time of united prayer and praise when they brought before the Lord the matters which at the time called for thanksgiving and supplication.

Mrs. Müeller had never been a very healthy woman, and more than once had been brought nigh unto death. In October, 1859, after twenty-nine years of wedded life and love, she had been laid aside by rheumatism and had continued in great suffering for about nine months, quite helpless and unable to work. But it was felt to be a special mark of God's love and faithfulness that this very affliction was used by Him to reestablish her in health and strength, the compulsory rest made necessary for the greater part of a year being in Mr. Müeller's judgment a means of prolonging her life and period of service for the ten years following. Thus a severe trial met by them both in faith had issued in much blessing both to soul and body.

The closing scenes of this beautiful life are almost too sacred to be unveiled to common eyes. For some few years before her departure, it was plain that her health and vitality were declining. It was difficult to prevail upon her to abate her activity, or even when a distressing cough attacked her, to allow a physician to be called. Her husband carefully guarded and nursed her, and by careful attention to diet and rest, avoidance of needless exposure, and by constant resort to prayer, she was kept alive through much weakness and sometimes much pain. But, on Saturday night, February 5th, she found that she did not have the use of one of her limbs, and it was obvious that the end was nigh. Her own mind was clear and her own heart at peace. She herself remarked, "He will soon come." And a few minutes after four in the afternoon of the Lord's Day, February 6, 1870, she sweetly passed from human toils and trials to be forever with the Lord.

Under the weight of such a sorrow, most men would have sunk into depths of almost hopeless despair. But this man of God, sustained by a divine love, at once sought for occasions of thanksgiving. Instead of repining over his loss, he gratefully remembered and recorded the goodness of God in *taking* such a wife, releasing her saintly spirit from the bondage of weakness, sickness, and pain, rather than leaving her to a protracted suffering and the mute agony of helplessness; and, above all, introducing her to her heart's desire, the immediate presence of the Lord Jesus, and the higher service of a celestial sphere. Is that not grief akin to selfishness which dwells so much on our own deprivations as to be oblivious of the ecstatic gain of the departed saints who, withdrawn from us and absent from the body, are at home with the Lord?

It is only in those circumstances of extreme trial which prove to ordinary men a crushing weight, that implicit faith in the Father's unfailing wisdom and love proves its full power to sustain. Where self-will is truly lost in the will of God, the life that is hidden in Him is most radiantly exhibited in the darkest hour.

The death of this beloved wife afforded an illustration of this. Within a few hours after this withdrawal of her who had shared with him the planning and working of these long years of service, Mr. Müeller went to the Monday evening prayer meeting in Salem Chapel to mingle his prayers and praises as usual with those of his brethren.

With a literally shining countenance, he rose and said: "Beloved brethren and sisters in Christ, I ask you to join with me in hearty praise and thanksgiving to my precious Lord for His loving kindness in having taken my darling, beloved wife out of the pain and suffering which she has endured, into His own presence, and as I rejoice in everything that is for her happiness. So I now rejoice as I realize how far happier she is in beholding her Lord, whom she loved so well, than in any joy she has known or could know here. I ask you also to pray that the Lord will so enable me to have fellowship in her joy that my bereaved heart may be occupied with her blessedness instead of my unspeakable loss."

These remarkable words are supplied by one who was himself present and on whose memory they made an indelible impression.

This occurrence had a marked effect upon all who were at that meeting. Mrs. Müeller was known by all as a most valuable, lovely, holy woman and wife. After nearly forty years of wedded life and love, she had left the earthly home for the heavenly. To her husband she had been a blessing beyond description, and to her daughter Lydia, at once a wise and tender mother and a sympathetic companion. The loss to them both could never be made up on Earth. Yet in these circumstances this man of God had grace given to forget his own and his daughter's irreparable loss, and to praise God for the unspeakable gain to the departed wife and mother.

The body was laid to rest on February 11th, many thousands of sorrowing friends evincing the deepest sympathy. Twelve hundred orphans mingled in the funeral procession, and the whole staff of helpers, as many as could be spared from the houses. The bereaved husband strangely upheld by the arm of the Almighty Friend in whom he trusted, took upon himself the funeral service both at chapel and cemetery. He was taken seriously ill afterward, but, as soon as his returning strength allowed, he preached his wife's funeral sermon—another memorable occasion. It was the supernatural serenity of his peace in the presence of such a bereavement that led his attending physician to say to a friend,

"I have never before seen so *unhuman* a man."

Yes, *un*human indeed though far from *in*human. He was lifted above the weakness of mere humanity by a power not of man. That funeral sermon was a noble tribute to the goodness of the Lord even in the great affliction of his life. The text was:

"Thou art good and doest good."
(Psalm 119:68)

Its three divisions were: "The Lord was good and did good: first, in giving her to me; second in leaving her so long to me; and third, in taking her from me."

It is happily presented in Mr. Müeller's journal, and must be read to be appreciated. This union, begun in prayer, was in prayer sanctified to the end. Mrs. Müeller's chief excellence lay in her devoted piety. She wore that one ornament which is in the sight of God of great price—the meek and quiet spirit; the beauty of the Lord her God was upon her. She had sympathetically shared her husband's prayers and tears during all the long trial time of faith and patience, and partaken of all the joys and rewards of the triumph hours. Mr. Müeller's own witness to her leaves nothing more to be added, for it is the tribute of him who knew her longest and best. He writes:

"She was God's own gift, exquisitely suited to me even in natural temperament. Thousands of times I said to her, 'My darling, God himself singled you out for me, as the most suitable wife I could possibly wish to have had.'"

As to culture, she had a basis of sensible practical education, surmounted and adorned by ladylike accomplishments which she had neither time nor inclination to indulge in her married life. Not only was she skilled in the languages and in such higher studies as astronomy, but in mathematics also. This last qualification made her an invaluable help to her husband for thirty-four years, as month by month she examined all the account books, and the hundreds of bills of the matrons of the orphan houses with the eye of an expert detecting the least mistake.

All her training and natural fitness indicated a providential adaptation to her work, like "the round peg in the round hole." Her practical education in needlework, and her knowledge of the material most serviceable for various household uses, made her competent to direct both in the purchase and manufacture of cloth and other fabrics for garments, bed linen, etc. She moved about those orphan houses like an angel of love, taking unselfish delight in such humble ministries as preparing neat, clean, beds to rest the little ones, and covering them with warm blankets in cold weather. For the sake of Him who took little children in His arms, she became to these thousands of destitute orphans a nursing mother.

Shortly after her death, a letter was received from a believing orphan sent out to service seventeen years before, asking also in behalf of others formerly in the houses, for permission to erect a stone over Mrs. Müeller's grave as an expression of love and grateful remembrance. Consent being given, hundreds of little offerings came in from orphans who during the twenty-five years previous had been under her motherly oversight, a beautiful tribute to her worth and a touching offering from those who had been to her as her larger family.

The dear daughter Lydia had, two years before Mrs. Müeller's departure, found in one of her mother's pocketbooks a sacred memorandum in her own writing, which she brought to her bereaved father's notice two days after his wife had departed. It belongs among the precious relics of her history. It reads as follows:

"Should it please the Lord to remove Mrs. Mary Müeller by a sudden dismissal, let none of the beloved survivors consider that it is in the way of judgment, either to her or to them. She has so often, when enjoying conscious nearness to the Lord, felt 'How sweet it would be now to depart and to be *forever* with Jesus,' that nothing but the shock it would be to her beloved husband and child, etc., has checked in her the longing desire that thus her happy spirit might take its flight. Precious Jesus! Thy will in this as in everything else, and not hers, be done!"

These words were to Mr. Müeller her last legacy; and with the comfort they gave him, the loving sympathy of his precious Lydia who did all that a daughter could do to fill a mother's place, and with the remembrance of Him who hath said,

"I will never leave thee nor forsake thee,"
he went on his lonely pilgrim way, rejoicing in the Lord,
feeling nevertheless a wound in his heart, which
seemed rather to deepen than to heal.

Sixteen months passed, when Mr. James Wright, who like Mr. Müeller had been bereft of his companion, asked of him the hand of the beloved Lydia in marriage. The request took Mr. Müeller wholly by surprise, but he felt that to no man living could he with more joyful confidence commit and entrust his choicest remaining earthly treasure. Ever solicitous for others' happiness rather than his own, he encouraged his daughter to accept Mr. Wright's proffered love, when she naturally hesitated on her father's account. On November 16, 1871, they were married and began a life of mutual prayer and sympathy like that of her father and mother, which proved supremely and almost ideally happy, helpful, and useful.

While as yet this event was still being planned, Mr. Müeller felt his own lonely condition keenly, and much more in view of his daughter's expected departure to her husband's home. He felt the need of someone to share intimately his toils and prayers, and help him in the Lord's work, and the persuasion grew upon him that it was God's will that he should marry again. After much prayer, he determined to ask Miss Susannah Grace Sangar to become his wife having known her for more than twenty-five years as a consistent disciple, and believing her to be well fitted to be his helper in the Lord. Accordingly, fourteen days after his daughter's marriage to Mr. Wright, he entered into similar relations with Miss Sangar, who for years after joined him in prayer, unselfish giving, and labors for souls.

The second Mrs. Müeller was of one mind with her husband as to the stewardship of the Lord's property. He found her poor, for what she had once possessed she had lost; and had she been rich he would have regarded her wealth as an obstacle to marriage, unfitting her to be his companion in a self-denial based on scriptural principle. Riches or hoarded wealth would have been to both of them a snare, and so having still, before her marriage, a remnant of two hundred pounds, she at once put it at the Lord's disposal, thus joining her husband in a life of voluntary poverty Although subsequent legacies were paid to her, she continued to the day of her death to be poor for the Lord's sake.

The question had often been asked Mr. Müeller what would become of the *work* when he, the master workman, would be removed. Men find it hard to get their eyes off the instrument, and remember that there is strictly speaking, only one AGENT, for an agent is *one who works,* and an instrument is what *the agent works with.* Though provision might be made in a board of trustees for carrying on the orphan work, where would be found the man to take the direction of it, a man whose spirit was so akin to that of the founder that he would trust in God and depend on Him just as Mr. Müeller had done? Such were the inquiries of the somewhat doubtful or fearful observers of the great and many branched work carried on under Mr. Müeller's supervision.

To all such questions he had always one answer ready— his one uniform solution of all cares and perplexities: *the Living God.* He who had built the orphan houses could maintain them; He who had raised up one humble man to oversee the work in His name, could provide for a worthy successor, like Joshua who not only *followed* but *succeeded* Moses. Jehovah of hosts is not limited in resources.

Nevertheless much prayer was offered that the Lord would provide such a successor, and, in Mr. James Wright, the prayer was answered. He was not chosen as Mr. Müeller's son-in-law; for the choice was made before his marriage to Lydia Müeller was even thought of by him. For more than thirty years, even from his boyhood, Mr. Wright had been well known to Mr. Müeller, and his growth in the things of God had been watched by him. For thirteen years he had already been his "right hand" in all most important matters; and for nearly all of that time had been held up before God as his successor in the prayers of Mr. and Mrs. Müeller, both of whom felt divinely assured that God would fit him more and more to take the entire burden of responsibility.

In 1870 ,when his wife fell asleep in Jesus, and Mr. Müeller was himself ill that he opened his heart to Mr. Wright as to the succession. Humility led him to shrink from such a post, and his then wife feared it would prove too burdensome for him; but all objections were overborne when it was seen and felt to be God's call. It was twenty-one months after this in November, 1871, Mr. Wright was married to Mr. Müller's only daughter and child, so that it is quite apparent that he had neither sought the position he now occupies, nor was he appointed to it because he was Mr. Müeller's son-in-law, for at that time, his first wife was living and in health. Therefore, from May, 1872, Mr. Wright shared with his father-in-law the responsibilities of the Institution, and gave him great joy as a partner and successor in full sympathy with all the great principles on which his work had been based.

A little over three years after Mr. Müeller's second marriage, in March, 1874, Mrs. Müeller was taken ill, and two days later became feverish and restless, and after about two weeks was attacked with a hemorrhage that brought her very near to the gates of death. She rallied; but fever and delirium followed and obstinate sleeplessness, until for a second time, she seemed at the point of death. Indeed so low was her vitality that, as late as April 17th, a most experienced London physician said that he had never known any patient to recover from such an illness; and thus a third time all human hope of restoration seemed gone. And yet, in answer to prayer, Mrs. Müeller was raised up and was taken to the seaside in the end of May for change of air, where she rapidly grew stronger until she was entirely restored. Thus the Lord spared her to be the companion of her husband in those years of missionary touring which enabled him to bear such world-wide witness. Out of the shadow of his griefs this beloved man of God ever came to find that divine refreshment which is as the *"shadow of a great rock in a weary land"* (Isaiah 32:2b).

Quotes & Notes from Well-Known Christians

THE LIFE AND MINISTRY of George Müeller inspired the following quotes and notes from these well-known Christians.

"The power of prayer was central to the ministry of George Müeller as he founded, built, and operated his orphan houses in nineteenth-century England. The narrative account of God's dealings with this pillar of prayer will challenge you to discover the secret of believing prayer for yourself."—**A.E.C Brooks**

"George Müeller (1805-1898), evangelist and philanthropist in England, was a man of prayer and strong faith who depended wholly on God for his temporal and spiritual needs." —**A.E.C. Brooks**

"When God wishes anew to teach His Church a truth that is not being understood or practiced, He mostly does so by raising some man to be raised up in this nineteenth century, among others, George Müeller to be His witness that He is indeed the Hearer of prayer. I know of no way in which the principal truths of God's Word in regard to prayer can be more effectually illustrated and established than a short review of his life and of what he tells of his prayer-experiences."—**Andrew Murray on George Müeller**

"(One of his four rules was :) Never to ask any human being for help, however great the need might be, but to make his wants known to the God who has promised to care for His servants and to hear their prayer." —**Andrew Murray on George Müeller**

"Of flowers of speech he has none, and we hardly think he cares for them; but of the bread of Heaven he has abundance." —**Charles Spurgeon on George Müeller**

The terms "Faith Ministry," "Living On Faith," "Living on Prayer," and similar descriptive phrases all go back to George Müeller, who made the decision to found and operate his many ministries (including hundreds of schools and several orphanages, eventually with thousands of children) without ever asking anyone other than God for money. During his lifetime he received (and gave away) over $7,200,000 dollars (in 1890's era money) through prayer alone.

Read almost any book about prayer, and the name George Müeller comes up. Many of our *Prayer Heroes* were inspired by his life with God. *Rees Howells* was, *R.A. Torrey* was *Charles Spurgeon* was, *L'Abri Fellowship* was and still is, and *Hank Hanegraaff (The Bible Answer Man)* quotes him in his book *The Covering.* We were at first influenced by him through *Rees Howels,* and then through reading about his own life directly." —**The Prayer Foundation**

"Reading without meditation is unfruitful; meditation without reading is hurtful; to meditate and to read without prayer upon both is without blessing." —**William Bridge, Puritan Writer**

"One of the mightiest men of prayer of the last generation was George Müeller of Bristol, England, who in the last sixty years of his life (he lived to be ninety-two or ninety-three) obtained the English equivalent of $7.200, 000.00 by prayer, But George Müeller never prayed for a thing just because he wanted it, or even just because he felt it was greatly needed for God's work. When it was laid upon George Müeller's heart to pray for anything, he would search the Scriptures to find if there was some promise that covered the case. Sometimes he would search the Scriptures for days before he presented his petition to God. And then when he found the promise, with his open Bible before him, and his finger upon that promise, he would plead that promise, and so he received what he asked. He always prayed with an open Bible before him." —**R. A. Torrey on George Müeller; "The Power of Prayer," 1924 (P.81)**

"The work of George Müeller in Bristol, England, was a miracle of the nineteenth century. It will take the opening of the books at the great judgment day to disclose all he wrought through prayer. This godly man never asked anyone for money for running expenses at his orphanage where hundreds of fatherless and motherless children were cared for. His practice was always to ask God for just what was need, and the answers which came to him read just like a record of apostolic times.

"He prayed for everything and trusted implicitly to God to supply all of his needs. And it is a matter of record that never did he and the orphans ever lack for any good thing." —**E. M. Bounds**

"One night when all the household had retired Müeller asked me to join him in prayer. He told me that there was absolutely nothing in the house for next morning's breakfast. I tried to remonstrate with him and to remind him that all the stores were closed. Müeller knew all that. He had prayed as he always prayed, and he never told anyone of his needs but God. We prayed—at least Müeller did—and I tried to. We went to bed and slept, and breakfast *for two thousand children was there in abundance at the usual breakfast hour.* Neither Müeller nor I ever knew how the answer came. The story was told next morning to Simon Short of Bristol, under pledge of secrecy until the benefactor died. The details of it are thrilling, but all that need be told here is that the Lord called him out of bed in the middle of the night to send breakfast to Müeller's orphanage, and knowing nothing of the need, or of the two men at prayer, he sent provisions that would feed them a month."

—Dr. A. T. Pierson

"When I first came to America thirty-one years ago, I crossed the Atlantic with the captain of a steamer who was one of the most devoted men I ever knew; and when we were off the banks of Newfoundland he said to me: 'Mr. Inglis, the last time I crossed here, five weeks ago, one of the most extraordinary things happened that has completely revolutionized the whole of my Christian life. Up to that time I was one of your ordinary Christians. We had a man of God on board, George Müeller, of Bristol. I had been on that bridge for twenty-two hours and never left it. I was startled by someone tapping me on the shoulder. It was George Müeller.

"'Captain,' said he, 'I have come to tell you that I must be in Quebec on Saturday afternoon.' This was Wednesday.

"'It is impossible,' I said.

"'Very well, if your ship can't take me God will find some other means of locomotion to take me. I have never broken an engagement in fifty-seven years.'

"'I would willingly help you, but how can I? I am helpless.'

"'Let us go down to the chart room and pray,' he said.

"I looked at this man and I thought to myself, 'What lunatic asylum could the man have come from? I never heard of such a thing.'

"'Mr. Müeller,' I said, 'do you know how dense this fog is?'

"'No,' he replied, 'my eye is not on the density of the fog, but on the living God, who controls every circumstance of my life.'

"'He went down on his knees, and he prayed one of the most simple prayers. I thought to myself, 'That would suit a children's class, where the children were not more than eight or nine years of age.' The burden of his prayer was something like this: 'O Lord, if it is consistent with

Thy will, please remove this fog in five minutes. You
know the engagement You made for me in Quebec for
Saturday. I believe it is Your will.'

"When he had finished, I was going to pray, but he put
his hand on my shoulder and told me not to pray.

"'First,' he said, 'you do not believe God will do it;
and, second, I believe He has done it. And there is no need
whatever for you to pray about it.'

"I looked at him, and George Müeller said this:
'Captain, I have known my Lord for fifty-seven years and
there has never been a single day that I have failed to gain
an audience with the King. Get up, Captain and open the
door, and you will find the fog is gone.' I got up, and the
fog was gone. On Saturday afternoon George Müeller was
in Quebec." —**Charles Inglis, Evangelist**

When asked him if he spent much time on his knees
in prayer, Müeller replied: "Hours every day. But I live in
the spirit of prayer; I pray as I walk, when I lie down, and
when I rise. And the answers are always coming. Tens of
thousands of times my prayers have been answered. When
once I am persuaded a thing is right, I go on praying for
it until the end comes. I never give up!"

"In answer to my prayers, thousands of souls have
been saved," he went on. "I shall meet tens of thousands
of them in Heaven."

There was another pause. I made no remark and he
continued: "The great point is to never give up until the
answer comes. I have been praying every day for fifty-two
years for two men, sons of a friend of my youth. They
are not converted yet, but they will be! How can it be
otherwise? There is the unchanging promise of Jehovah, and
on that I rest. The great fault of the children of God is that
they do not continue in prayer; they do not go on praying;
they do not persevere. If they desire anything of God's glory,

they should pray until they get it. [I read somewhere long ago that both men were saved at Müeller›s funeral, where an altar call was made. They both went to the altar at the same time, though they did not know each other.]

"Oh, how good, kind, gracious, and condescending is the One with whom we have to do! He has given me, unworthy as I am, immeasurably above all I have asked or thought! I am only a poor, frail, sinful man, but He has heard my prayers tens of thousands of times and used me as the means of bringing tens of thousands of souls into the way of truth in this and other lands. These unworthy lips have proclaimed salvation to great multitudes, and very many people have believed unto eternal life."

"Seek to depend entirely on God for everything," he answered. "Put yourself and your work into His hands. When thinking of any new undertaking, ask, Is this agreeable to the mind of God? Is it for His glory? If it is not for His glory, it is not for your good, and you must have nothing to do with it. Mind that! Having settled that a certain course is for the glory of God, begin it in His name and continue in it to the end. Undertake it in prayer and faith, and never give up!"

"And do not regard iniquity in your heart. If you do, the Lord will not hear you. Keep that before you always. Then trust in God. Depend only on Him. Wait on Him. Believe on Him. Expect great things from Him. Faint not if the blessing tarries. And above all, rely only on the merits of our adorable Lord and Savior, so that according to them and to nothing of your own, the prayers you offer and the work you do be accepted. —**Pastor Charles R. Parsons**

ANDREW MURRAY'S ACCOUNT OF THE SECRET OF GEORGE MÜELLER'S POWER IN PRAYER

WHEN God wishes to teach His Church a truth that is not being understood or practiced, He most often does so by raising some man to be a living witness to its blessedness in word and deed.

So in this nineteenth century, God has raised up, among others, George Müeller to be His witness that He is indeed the Hearer of prayer. I know of no way in which the principal truths of God's Word in regard to prayer can be more effectually illustrated and established than in a short review of his life and what he tells of his experiences in prayer.

A few extracts in regard to his spiritual life will prepare the way for what we especially wish to quote of his experiences in reference to prayer:

"In connection with this I would mention, that the Lord very graciously gave me, from the very commencement of my divine life, a measure of simplicity and of childlike disposition in spiritual things. Although I was exceedingly ignorant of the Scriptures, and was still from time to time overcome by outward sin, yet I was enabled to carry most minute matters to the Lord in prayer. And I have found "... *godliness is profitable unto all things, having promise of the life that now is, and of that which is to come*" (1 Timothy 4:8). Though very weak and ignorant, yet I had now, by the grace of God, some desire to benefit others, and he who so faithfully had once served Satan, sought now to win souls for Christ."

It was at Teignmouth that he was led to know how to

use God's word, and to trust the Holy Spirit as the Teacher given by God to make that word clear. He writes:

"God then began to show me that the Word of God alone is our standard of judgment in spiritual things; that it can be explained only by the Holy Spirit; and that in our day, as well as in former times. He is the Teacher of His people. The office of the Holy Spirit I had not experimentally understood before that time.

'It was my beginning to understand this latter point in particular, which had a great effect on me. For the Lord enabled me to put it to the test of experience, by laying aside commentaries, and almost every other book and simply reading the Word of God and studying it.

'The result of this was, that the first evening I shut myself into my room to give myself to prayer and meditation over the Scriptures, I learned more in a few hours than I had done during a period of several months previously.

'But the particular difference was that I received real strength for my soul in so doing. I now began to try by the test of the Scriptures the things which I had learned and seen, and found that only those principles which stood the test were of real value."

Of obedience to the Word of God, he writes as follows, in connection with his being baptized:

"It had pleased God, in His abundant mercy, to bring my mind into such a state, that I was willing to carry out into my life whatever I found in the Scriptures. I could say, 'I will do His will,' and it was on that account, I believe, that I saw which doctrine is of God. And I would observe here, by the way, that the passage to which I have just alluded (John 7:17) has been a most remarkable comment to me on many doctrines and precepts of our most holy faith."

"For instance: *'Resist not evil; but whosoever shall smite thee on thy right cheek, turn to him the other also. And if any man will sue thee at the law, and take away thy coat, let him have thy cloak also. And whosoever shall compel thee to go a mile, go with him twain. Give to him that asketh thee, and from him that would borrow of thee, turn not thou away. Love your enemies, bless them that curse you, do good to them that hate you, and pray for them which despitefully use you, and persecute you"* (Matthew 5:39-44). *"Sell that ye have, and give alms"* (Luke 12:33). *"Owe no man any thing, but to love one another"* (Romans 13:8).

'It may be said, "Surely these passages cannot be taken literally, for how then would the people of God be able to pass through the world? The state of mind enjoined in John 7:17 will cause such objections to vanish. Whosoever is willing to act out these commandments of the Lord *literally*, will, I believe, be led with me to see that to take them *literally* is the will of God. Those who do so will doubtless often be brought into difficulties hard for the flesh to bear. But these will have a tendency to make them constantly feel that they are strangers and pilgrims here, and that this world is not their home. Therefore, throwing them more upon God, who will assuredly help them through any difficulty into which they may be brought by seeking to act in obedience to His Word."

This implicit surrender to God's Word led him to certain views and conduct in regard to money, which mightily influenced his future life. They had their root in the conviction that money was a Divine stewardship, and that all money had therefore to be received and dispensed in direct fellowship with God himself.

This led him to the adoption of the following four great rules:

1. Not to receive any fixed salary, both because in the collecting of it there was often much that was at

variance with the freewill offering with which God's service is to be maintained, and in the receiving of it a danger of placing more dependence on human sources of income than in the living God himself.

2. Never to ask any human being for help, however great the need might be, but to make his wants known to the God who has promised to care for His servants and to hear their prayer.

3. To take this command in Luke 12:33 literally, *Sell that thou hast and give alms,* and never to save up money, but to spend all God entrusted to him on God's poor, on the work of His Kingdom.

4. Also to take Romans 18:8, *"Owe no man anything,"* literally, and never to buy on credit, or be in debt for anything, but to trust God to provide.

This mode of living was not easy at first. But Müeller testifies it was most blessed in bringing the soul to rest in God, and drawing it into closer union with Him when inclined to backslide. 'For it will not do, it is not possible, to live in sin, and at the same time, by communion with God, to draw down from heaven everything one needs for the life that now is.'

Not long after his settlement at Bristol, *The Scriptural Knowledge Institution for Home and Abroad'* was established for aiding in Day School, Sunday school, Mission and Bible work. Of this Institution the Orphan Home work, by which Mr. Müeller is best known, became a branch. It was in 1834 that his heart was touched by the case of an orphan brought to Christ in one of the schools, but who had to go to a poorhouse where its spiritual wants would not be cared for.

Meeting shortly after reading the life of August H. Franké, he writes on November 20, 1835: "Today I have had it very much laid on my heart no longer merely to think about the establishment of an Orphan Home, but actually to set about it, and I have been very much in prayer respecting it, in order to ascertain the Lord's mind. May God make it plain.' And again, Nov. 25: 'I have been again much in prayer yesterday and today about the Orphan Home, and am more and more convinced that it is of God. May He in mercy guide me. The three chief reasons are:

1. That God may be glorified, should He be pleased to furnish me with the means, in its being seen that it is not a vain thing to trust Him; and that thus the faith of His children may be strengthened.

2. The spiritual welfare of fatherless and motherless children.

3. Their temporal welfare.

After some months of prayer and waiting on God, a house was rented, with room for thirty children, and in course of time three more, containing in all 120 children. The work was carried on it this way for ten years, the supplies for the needs of the orphans being asked and received of God alone. It was often a time of sore need and much prayer, but a trial of faith more precious than of gold was found unto praise and honor and glory of God. The Lord was preparing His servant for greater things. By His providence and His Holy Spirit, Mr. Müeller was led to desire, and to wait upon God till he received from Him, the sure promise of £15,000 for an Orphan Home to contain 300 children. This first Orphan Home was opened in 1849. In 1858, a second and third Orphan Home, for 950 more orphans, was opened, costing £35,000. And in 1869 and 1870, a fourth and a fifth Orphan Home, for 850 more, at an expense of £50,000, making the total number of the orphan children to be 2100.

In addition to this work, God has given him almost as much as for the building of the Orphan Homes, and the maintenance of the orphans, for other work, the support of schools and missions, Bible and tract circulation. In all he has received from God, to be spent in His work, during these fifty years, more than one million pounds sterling. How little he knew, let us carefully notice, that when he gave up his little salary of £35 a year in obedience to the leading of God's word and the Holy Spirit, what God was preparing to give him as the reward of obedience and faith; and how wonderfully the word was to be fulfilled to him: *"Thou hast been faithful over few things; I will set thee over many things"* (Matthew 25:21).

And these things have happened for an example to us. God calls us to be followers of George Müeller, even as he is of Christ. His God is our God; the same promises are for us; the same service of love and faith in which he labored is calling for us on every side. Let us in connection with our lessons in the school of prayer study the way in which God gave George Müeller such power as a man of prayer: we shall find in it the most remarkable illustration of some of the lessons which we have been studying with the blessed Master in the word. We shall specially have impressed upon us His first great lesson, that if we will come to Him in the way He has pointed out, with definite petitions, made known to us by the Spirit through the word as being according to the will of God, we may most confidently believe that whatsoever we ask it shall be done.

PRAYER AND THE WORD OF GOD

We have more than once seen that God's listening to our voice depends upon our listening to His voice. We must not only have a special promise to plead, when we make a special request, but our whole life must be under the supremacy of the Word: the Word must be dwelling in us. The testimony of George Müeller on this point is most instructive. He tells us how the discovery of the true place of the Word of God, and the teaching of the Spirit with it, was the commencement of a new era in his spiritual life. Of it he writes: "Now the scriptural way of reasoning would have been: God himself has condescended to become an author, and I am ignorant about that precious book which His Holy Spirit has caused to be written through the instrumentality of His servants, and it contains that which I ought to know, and the knowledge of which will lead me to true happiness; therefore I ought to read again and again this most precious book, this book of books, most earnestly, most prayerfully, and with much meditation; and in this practice I ought to continue all the days of my life.

'For I was aware, though I read it but little, that I knew scarcely anything of it. But instead of acting thus and being led by my ignorance of the Word of God to study it more, my difficulty in understanding it, and the little enjoyment I had in it, made me careless of reading it (for much prayerful reading of the Word gives not merely more knowledge, but increases the delight we have in reading it); and thus, like many believers, I practically preferred, for the first four years of my divine life, the works of uninspired men to the oracles of the living God. The consequence was that I remained a babe, both in knowledge and grace. In knowledge, I say; for all true knowledge must be derived, by the Spirit, from the Word. And as I neglected the Word, I was for nearly four years so ignorant, that I did not clearly know even the fundamental points of our holy faith. And this lack of knowledge most sadly kept me back from walking steadily in the ways of God.

'For when it pleased the Lord in August 1829 to bring me really to the Scriptures, my life and walk became very different. And though ever since that I have very much fallen short of what I might and ought to be, yet by the grace of God I have been enabled to live much nearer to Him than before. If any believers read this who in practice prefer other books to the Holy Scriptures, and who enjoy the writings of men much more than the word of God, may they be warned by my loss. I shall consider this book to have been the means of doing much good, should it please the Lord, through its instrumentality, to lead some of His people no longer to neglect the Holy Scriptures, but to give them that preference which they have hitherto bestowed on the writings of men.

'Before I leave this subject, I would only add: If the reader understands very little of the Word of God, he ought to read it very much; for the Spirit explains the Word by the Word. And if he enjoys the reading of the Word little, that is just the reason why he should read it much; for the frequent reading of the Scriptures creates a delight in them, so that the more we read them, the more we desire to do so.

'Above all, he should seek to have it settled in his own mind that God alone by His Spirit can teach him, and that therefore, as God will be inquired of for blessings, it becomes him to seek God's blessing previous to reading, and also whilst reading.

'He should have it, moreover, settled in his mind that although the Holy Spirit is the best and sufficient Teacher, yet that this Teacher does not always teach immediately when we desire it, and that therefore we may have to entreat Him again and again for the explanation of certain passages; but that He will surely teach us at last, if indeed we are seeking for light prayerfully, patiently, and with a view to the glory of God." The extracts are from a work in four volumes, The Lord's Dealings with George Müeller, J. Nisbet & Co., London.

We find in his journal frequent mention made of his spending two and three hours in prayer over the Word for the feeding of his spiritual life. As the fruit of this, when he had need of strength and encouragement in prayer, the individual promises were not to him so many arguments from a book to be used with God, but living words which he had heard the Father's living voice speak to him, and which he could now bring to the Father in living faith.

PRAYER AND THE WILL OF GOD

One of the greatest difficulties with young believers is to know how they can find out whether what they desire is according to God's will. I count it one of the most precious lessons God wants to teach through the experience of George Müeller, that He is willing to make known, of things of which His Word says nothing directly, that they are His will for us, and that we may ask them. The teaching of the Spirit, not without or against the Word, but as something above and beyond it, in addition to it, without which we cannot see God's will, is the heritage of every believer. It is through *the Word and the Word of Alone* that the Spirit teaches, applying the general principles or promises to our special need. And it is the Spirit, and the Spirit Alone, who can really make the Word a light on our path, whether the path of duty in our daily walk, or the path of faith in our approach to God. Let us try and notice in what childlike simplicity and teachableness it was that the discovery of God's will was so surely and so clearly made known to His servant.

With regard to the building of the first Home and the assurance he had of its being God's will, he writes in May 1850, just after it had been opened, speaking of the great difficulties there were, and how little likely it appeared to nature that they would be removed: "But while the prospect before me would have been overwhelming had I looked at it naturally, I was never even for once permitted to question how it would end. For as from the beginning I was sure it was the will of God that I should go to the work of building for Him this large Orphan Home, so also from the beginning I was as certain that the whole would be finished as if the Home had been already filled."

The way in which he found out what was God's will, comes out with special clearness in his account of the building of the second Home; and I ask the reader to study with care the lesson the narrative conveys:

"December 5, 1850: Under these circumstances I can only pray that the Lord in His tender mercy would not allow Satan to gain an advantage over me. By the grace of God my heart says: Lord, if I could be sure that it is Thy will that I should go forward in this matter, I would do so cheerfully; and, on the other hand, if I could be sure that these are vain, foolish, proud thoughts, that they are not from Thee, I would, by Thy grace, hate them, and entirely put them aside.

'My hope is in God: He will help and teach me. Judging, however, from His former dealings with me, it would not be a strange thing to me, nor surprising, if He called me to labor yet still more largely in this way.

'The thoughts about enlarging the Orphan work have not yet arisen on account of an abundance of money having lately come in; for I have had of late to wait for about seven weeks upon God, while little, very little comparatively, came in, i.e. about four times as much was going out as came in; and, had not the Lord previously sent me large sums, we should have been distressed indeed.

'Lord! How can your servant know your will in this matter? Will you be pleased to teach him"?

"December 11: During the last six days, since writing

the above, I have been, day after day, waiting upon God concerning this matter. It has generally been more or less all the day on my heart. When I have been awake at night, it has not been far from my thoughts. Yet all this without the least excitement. I am perfectly calm and quiet respecting it. My soul would be rejoiced to go forward in this service, could I be sure that the Lord would have me to do so; for then, notwithstanding the numberless difficulties, all would be well; and His name would be magnified.

'On the other hand, were I assured that the Lord would have me to be satisfied with my present sphere of service, and that I should not pray about enlarging the work, by His grace I could, without an effort, cheerfully yield to it; for He has brought me into such a state of heart, that I only desire to please Him in this matter. Moreover, hitherto I have not spoken about this thing even to my beloved wife, the sharer of my joys, sorrows, and labors for more than twenty years; nor is it likely that I shall do so for some time to come: for I prefer quietly to wait on the Lord, without conversing on this subject, in order that thus I may be kept the more easily, by His blessing, from being influenced by things from without. The burden of my prayer concerning this matter is that the Lord would not allow me to make a mistake, and that He would teach me to do His will."

"December 26: Fifteen days have elapsed since I wrote the preceding paragraph. Every day since then I have continued to pray about this matter and that with a goodly measure of earnestness, by the help of God. There has passed scarcely an hour during these days, in which, while awake, this matter has not been more or less before me. But all without even a shadow of excitement. I converse with no one about it not even have I not even done so with my dear wife. For this I refrain still, and deal with God alone about the matter, in order that no outward influence and no outward excitement may keep me from attaining unto a clear discovery of His will. I have the fullest and most peaceful assurance that He will clearly show me His will.

'This evening I have had again an especially solemn season for prayer, to seek to know the will of God. But while I continue to earnestly pray and beseech the Lord, that He would not allow me to be deluded in this business, I may say I have scarcely any doubt remaining on my mind as to what will be the issue, even that I should go forward in this matter. As this, however, is one of the most momentous steps that I have ever taken, I judge that I cannot go about this matter with too much caution, prayerfulness, and deliberation. I am in no hurry about it. I could wait for years, by God's grace, were this His will, before even taking one single step toward this thing, or even speaking to anyone about it; and, on the other hand, I would set to work tomorrow, were the Lord to bid me do so. This calmness of mind, this having no will of my own in the matter, this only wishing to please my Heavenly Father in it, this only seeking His and not my honor in it; this state of heart, I say, is the fullest assurance to me that my heart is not under a fleshly excitement, and that, if I am helped thus to go on, I shall know the will of God to the full. But, while I write this, I cannot but add at the same time, that I do crave the honor and the glorious privilege to be more and more used by the Lord.

'I desire to be allowed to provide scriptural instruction for a thousand orphans, instead of doing so for three hundred. I desire to expound the Holy Scriptures regularly to a thousand orphans, instead of doing so to three hundred. I desire that it may be yet more abundantly manifest that God is still the Hearer and Answerer of prayer, and that He is the living God now as He ever was and ever will be, when He shall simply, in answer to prayer, have condescended to provide me with a house for seven hundred orphans and with means to support them. This last consideration is the most important point in my mind. The Lord's honor is the principal point with me in this whole matter; and just because this is the case, if He would be more glorified by not going forward in this business, I should by His grace be perfectly content to give up all thoughts about another Orphan House. Surely in such a state of mind, obtained by the Holy Spirit, thou, O my heavenly Father, wilt not suffer thy child to be mistaken, much less deluded. By the help of God I shall continue further day by day to wait upon Him in prayer, concerning this thing, till He shall bid me act."

"January 2, 1851: A week ago I wrote the preceding paragraph. During this week I have still been helped day by day and more than once every day, to seek the guidance of the Lord about another Orphan House. The burden of my prayer has still been that He in His great mercy would keep me from making a mistake. During the last week the Book of Proverbs has come in the course of my Scripture reading, and my heart has been refreshed in reference to this subject by the following passages: *Trust in the Lord with all thine heart; and lean not unto thine own understanding. In all thy ways acknowledge Him, and He shall direct thy paths"* (Proverbs 3:5, 6). By the grace of God I do acknowledge the Lord in all my ways, and in this thing in particular; I have therefore the comfortable assurance that He will direct my paths concerning this part of my service, as to whether I shall be occupied in it or not. Further: *"The integrity of the upright shall preserve them"* (Proverbs 11:3). By the grace of God I am upright in this business. My honest purpose is to get glory to God. Therefore I expect to be guided aright. Further: *"Commit thy works unto the Lord, and thy thoughts shall be established"* (Proverbs 16:3). I do commit my works unto the Lord, and therefore expect that my thoughts will be established. My heart is more and more coming to a calm, quiet, and settled assurance that the Lord will condescend to use me still further in the orphan work. Here Lord is thy servant."

When later he decided to build two additional houses, Numbers 4 and 5, he writes thus again:

"Twelve days have passed away since I wrote the last paragraph. I have still day by day been enabled to wait upon the Lord with reference to enlarging the Orphan work, and have been during the whole of this period also in perfect peace, which is the result of seeking in this thing only the Lord's honor and the temporal and spiritual benefit of my fellow men. Without an effort could I by His grace put aside all thoughts about this whole affair, if only assured that it is the will of God that I should do so; and, on the other hand, would at once go forward, if He would have it be so. I have still kept this matter entirely to myself. Though it is now about seven weeks, since day by day, more or less, my mind has been exercised about it, and since I have been daily praying about it, yet not one human being knows of it. As yet I have not even mentioned it to my dear wife in order that thus, by quietly waiting upon God, I might not be influenced by what might be said to me on the subject. This evening has been particularly set apart for prayer, beseeching the Lord once more not to allow me to be mistaken in this thing, and much less to be deluded by the devil. I have also sought to let all the reasons against building another Orphan House, and all the reasons for doing so pass before my mind: and now for the clearness and definiteness, write them down. . . .

'Much, however, as the nine previous reasons weigh with me, yet they would not decide me if there were not one more. It is this. After having for months pondered the matter, and having looked at it in all its bearings and with all its difficulties, and then having been finally led, after much prayer, to decide on this enlargement, my mind is at peace. The child who has again and again sought his heavenly Father not to allow him to be deluded, nor even to make a mistake, is at peace, perfectly at peace concerning this decision; and has thus the assurance that the decision come to, after much prayer during weeks and months, is the leading of the Holy Spirit; and therefore purposes to go forward, assuredly believing that he will not be confounded, for he trusts in God. Many and great may be his difficulties; thousands and ten thousands of prayers may have ascended to God, before the full answer may be obtained; much exercise of faith and patience may be required; but in the end it will again be seen, that His servant, who trusts in Him, has not been confounded."

PRAYER AND THE GLORY OF GOD

We have sought more than once to enforce the truth, that while we ordinarily seek the reasons of our prayers not being heard in the thing we ask not being according to the will of God, Scripture warns us to find the cause in ourselves, in our not being in the right state or not asking in the right spirit. The thing may be in full accordance with His will, but the asking, the spirit of the supplicant, not; then we are not heard. As the great root of all sin is self and self-seeking, so there is nothing that even in our more spiritual desires so effectually hinders God in answering as this: we pray for our own pleasure or glory. Prayer to have power and prevail must ask for the glory of God; and he can only do this as he is living for God's glory.

In George Müeller, we have one of the most remarkable instances on record of God's Holy Spirit leading a man deliberately and systematically, at the outset of a course of prayer, to make the glorifying of God his first and only object. Let us ponder well what he says, and learn the lesson God would teach us through him:

"I had constantly cases brought before me, which proved that one of the special things which the children of God needed in our day, was to have their faith strengthened.

'I longed, therefore, to have something to point my brethren to, as a visible proof that our God and Father is the same faithful God as ever He was; as willing as ever to *prove* himself to be the Living God in our day as formerly, to all who put their trust in Him.

'My spirit longed to be instrumental in strengthening their faith, by giving them not only instances from the Word of God, of His willingness and ability to help all who rely upon Him, but to show them by proofs that He is the same in our day. I knew that the Word of God ought to be enough, and it was by grace enough for me; but still I considered I ought to lend a helping hand to my brethren.

'I therefore judged myself bound to be the servant of the Church of Christ, in the particular point in which I had obtained mercy; namely, in being able to take God at His Word and rely upon it. The first object of the work was, and is still: that God might be magnified by the fact that the orphans under my care are provided with all they need, only by prayer and faith, without any one being asked; thereby it may be seen that God is *faithful still, and hears prayers still.*

'I have again these last days prayed much about the Orphan House, and have frequently examined my heart; that if it were at all my desire to establish it for the sake of gratifying myself, I might find it out. For as I desire only the Lord's glory, I shall be glad to be instructed by the instrumentality of my brother, if the matter be not of Him.

'When I began the Orphan work in 1835, my chief object was the glory of God, by giving a practical demonstration as to what could be accomplished simply through the instrumentality of prayer and faith, in order thus to benefit the Church at large, and to lead a careless world to see the reality of the things of God, by showing them in this work, that the living God is still, as 4000 years ago, the living God. My aim has been abundantly honored. Multitudes of sinners have been thus converted; multitudes of the children of God in all parts of the world have been benefited by this work, even as I had anticipated. But the larger the work has grown, the greater has been the blessing, bestowed in the very way in which I looked for blessing: for the attention of hundreds of thousands has been drawn to the work; and many tens of thousands have come to see it. All this leads me to desire further and further to labor on in this way, in order to bring yet greater glory to the name of the Lord. That He may be looked at, magnified, admired, trusted in, relied on at all times, is my aim in this service; and so particularly in this intended enlargement. That it may be seen how much one poor man, simply by trusting in God, can bring about by prayer; and that thus other children of God may be led to carry on the work of God in dependence upon Him; and that children of God may be led increasingly to trust in Him in their individual positions and circumstances, therefore I am led to this further enlargement."

PRAYER AND TRUST IN GOD

There are other points on which I would be glad to point out what is to be found in Mr. Müeller's narrative, but one more must suffice. It is the lesson of firm and unwavering trust in God's promise as the secret of persevering prayer. If once we have, in submission to the teaching of the Spirit in the Word, taken hold of God's promise, and believed that the Father has heard us, we must not allow ourselves by any delay or unfavorable appearances be shaken in our faith.

"The full answer to my daily prayers was far from being realized; yet there was abundant encouragement granted by the Lord, to continue in prayer. But suppose, that far less had come in than was received, still, after having come to the conclusion upon scriptural grounds, and after much prayer and self-examination, I ought to have gone on without wavering, in the exercise of faith and patience concerning this object. Thus, when all the children of God, once satisfied that anything that they bring before God in prayer is according to His will, ought to continue in believing, expecting, persevering prayer until the blessing is granted. Thus, I am now myself waiting upon God for certain blessings, for which I have daily besought Him for ten years and six months without one day's intermission. Still the full answer is not yet given concerning the conversion of certain individuals, though in the meantime I have received many thousands of answers to prayer.

' I have also prayed daily without intermission for the conversion of other individuals about ten years, for others six or seven years, for others from three or two years; and still the answer is not yet granted concerning those persons, while in the meantime many thousands of my prayers have been answered, and also souls converted, for whom I had been praying. I lay particular stress on this for the benefit of those who may suppose that I need only to ask of God, and receive at once; or that I might pray concerning anything, and the answer would surely come. One can only expect to obtain answers to prayers that are according to the mind of God; and even then, patience and faith may be exercised for many years, even as mine are exercised, in the matter to which I have referred; and yet am I daily continuing in prayer, and expecting the answer, and so surely expecting the answer, that I have often thanked God that He will surely give it, though now for nineteen years faith and patience have thus been exercised. Be encouraged, dear Christians, with fresh earnestness to give yourselves to prayer, if you can only be sure that you ask things which are for the glory of God.

'But the most remarkable point is this, that £6, 6s. 6d. from Scotland supplied me, as far as can be known now, with all the means necessary for fitting up and promoting the New Orphan Houses. Six years and eight months I have been day by day, and generally several times daily, asking the Lord to give me the needed means for this enlargement of the Orphan work, which, according to calculations made in the spring of 1861, appeared to be about fifty thousand pounds: the total of this amount I had now received. I praise and magnify the Lord for putting this enlargement of the work into my heart, and for giving me courage and faith for it; and above all, for sustaining my faith day by day without wavering. When the last portion of the money was received, I was no more assured concerning the whole, than I was at the time I had not received one single donation towards this large sum. I was at the beginning, after once having ascertained His mind, through most patient and heart-searching waiting upon God, as fully assured that He would bring it about, as if the two houses, with their hundreds of orphans occupying them, had been already before me. I make a few remarks here for the sake of young believers in connection with this subject:

1. Be slow to take new steps in the Lord's service, in your business, or in your families: weigh everything well; weigh all in the light of the Holy Scriptures and in the fear of God.

2. Seek to have no will of your own, in order to ascertain the mind of God, regarding any steps you propose taking, so that you can honestly say you are willing to do the will of God, if He will only please to instruct you.

3. But when you have found out what the will of God is, seek for His help, and seek it earnestly, perseveringly, patiently, believingly, and expectantly; and you will surely in His own time and way obtain it.

'To suppose that we have difficulty about money only would be a mistake: there occur hundreds of other wants and other difficulties. It is a rare thing that a day occurs without some difficulty or some want; but often there are many difficulties and many wants to be met and overcome the same day. All these are met by prayer and faith, our universal remedy; and we have never been confounded. Patient, persevering, believing prayer, offered up to God, in the name of the Lord Jesus, has always, sooner or later, brought the blessing. I do not despair, by God's grace, of obtaining any blessing, provided I can be sure it would be for any real good, and for the glory of God."

ANSWERS TO PRAYER
FROM
GEORGE MÜELLER'S NARRATIVES

"I NEVER REMEMBER, in all my Christian course, a period now (in March, 1895) of sixty-nine years and four months, that I ever *sincerely* and *patiently* sought to know the will of God by the teaching of the Holy Ghost, through the instrumentality of the Word of God, but I have been *always* directed rightly. But if honesty of heart and uprightness before God were lacking or if I did not patiently wait upon God for instruction, or if I preferred the counsel of my fellow men to the declarations of the Word of the living God, I made great mistakes." —George Müeller

HOW TO ASCERTAIN THE WILL OF GOD

1. I seek at the beginning to get my heart into such a state that it has no will of its own in regard to a given matter. Nine tenths of the trouble people have with this is right here. Nine tenths of the difficulties are overcome when our hearts are ready to do the Lord's will, whatever it may be. When one is truly in this state, it is usually but a little way to the knowledge of what His will is.

2. Having done this, I do not leave the result to feeling or simple impression. If so, I make myself liable to great delusions.

3. I seek the Will of the Spirit of God through, or in connection with, the Word of God. The Spirit and the Word must be combined. If I look to the Spirit alone without the Word, I lay myself open to great delusions. If the Holy Ghost guides us at all, He will do it according to the Scriptures and never contrary to them.

4. Next I take into account providential circumstances. These often plainly indicate God's Will in connection with His Word and Spirit.

5. I ask God in prayer to reveal His Will to me rightly.

6. Thus, through prayer to God, the study of the Word, and reflection, I come to a deliberate judgment according to the best of my ability and knowledge, and if my mind is thus at peace, and continues so after two or three more petitions, I proceed accordingly. In trivial matters, and in transactions involving most important issues, I have found this method always effective.

—George Müeller

REASONS THAT LED
GEORGE MÜELLER TO ESTABLISH
ORPHAN HOMES

I CONSTANTLY had cases brought before me that proved that one special thing that children of God needed in our day was *to have their faith strengthened.*

For instance: I might visit a brother who worked fourteen or even sixteen hours a day at his trade, the necessary result of that was not only his body suffered, but his soul was lean, and he had no enjoyment in the things of God. Under such circumstances I might point out to him that he ought to work less, in order that his bodily health might not suffer, and that he might gather strength for his inner man by reading the Word of God, by meditating on it and by prayer. The reply was, however, I generally found to be something like this: "But if I work less, I do not enough to support my family. Even now, while I work so much, I have scarcely enough. The wages are low, and I must work hard in order to obtain what I need." There was no trust in god. No real belief in the truth of that Word: Seek ye first the kingdom of God, and His righteousness: and all these things shall be added unto you" (Matthew 6:33).

I might reply something like this: "My dear brother, it is not your work that supports your family, but the Lord; and He who has fed you and your family when you could not work at all on account of illness, for the sake of obtaining food for your inner man you were to work only for so many hours a day as would allow you proper time for rest. And is it not the case now that you begin your work of the day after having only a few hurried moments for prayer? And when you leave your work in the evening, and mean then to read a little of the Word of God, are you not too worn out in body and mind to enjoy it and therefore fall asleep while reading the Scriptures or while on your knees in prayer"? The brother would say it was so, he would agree that my advice was good; but still I read in his countenance, even though he did not say so, "How would I get on if I were to carry out your advice"? I longed to have something to point out to the brother as to a visible proof that our God and Father is the same faithful God as ever, and is willing as ever to prove himself to be the living God in our day as He was formerly to all who put their trust in Him. Also I found children of God tried in mind by the prospect of old age when they might not be able to work any longer, and therefore harassed by fear of having to go to the poorhouse. If in such a case I pointed out to them how their heavenly Father has always helped those who put their trust in Him, they might not, perhaps, always say that times have changed; but yet it was evident enough that God was not looked upon by them as the living God.

My spirit was oftentimes bowed down by this and I longed to set something before the children of God whereby they might see that He does not forsake, even in our day, those who rely upon Him. Another group of people were brethren in business who suffered in their souls and brought guilt on their consciences by carrying on their business almost in the same was as unconverted persons do. The competition in trade, the bad times, the overpopulation in the country, were given as reasons why if the business was carried on simply according to the Word of God it could not be expected to do well. Such a brother would express the wish that he might be differently situated; but very rarely did I see that there was a stand made for God. Nor was there a holy determination to trust in the living God, and to depend on Him in order for a good conscience to be maintained. To this group I likewise desire to show by visible proof that God is unchangeably the same.

Another group called professional people who could not continue with a good conscience or persons who were in an unscriptural position with reference to spiritual things; both classes feared because of consequences to give up the profession in which they could not abide in God, or to leave their position, lest they be thrown out of employment. My spirit longed to be instrumental in strengthening their faith by giving them not only instances from the Word of God of His willingness and ability to help all those who rely on Him, but to show them by proofs that He is the same in our day.

I knew very well that the Word of God ought to be enough, and it was by grace enough for me; but still, I considered that I ought to lend a helping hand to my brethren, if by any means; by the visible proof to the unchangeable faithfulness of the Lord I might strengthen their hands in God. I remembered what a great blessing my own soul had received through the Lord's dealing with His servant A. H. Francké, who in total dependence upon the living God alone, established an immense orphan home that I had seen many times with my own eyes.

I, therefore, judge myself bound to be the servant of the Church of God, in the particular point on which I had obtained mercy; namely, in being able to take God at His Word and to rely upon it. All these exercises of my soul, which resulted from the fact that so many believers with whom I was acquainted were distressed in mind, and guilty in their conscience on account of not trusting in the Lord; were used by God to awaken in my heart the desire of setting before the Church at large, and before the world, a proof that He has not in the least changed; and this seemed to be to be best done by the establishing of an orphan home. It needs to be something that could be seen, even by the natural eye.

Now if I, a poor man, simply by prayer and faith, obtained without asking any individual, the means for establishing and carrying on an orphan home, there would be something that with the Lord's blessing might be instrumental in strengthening the faith of the children of God. Also it would be a testimony to the consciences of the unconverted of the reality of the things of God. This was the primary reason for establishing the orphan homes. I certainly did from my own heart desire to be used by God to benefit the bodies of poor children without parents and seek with the help of God to do them good for this life. I also longed to be used of God to help train them up in the fear of God; but still the first and primary object of the work was (and still is) that God might be magnified by the fact that all the orphans under my care are provided with all they need only by prayer and faith, without anyone being asked by me or my fellow laborers how it may be seen that God is *faithful still and hears prayer still.*

The three chief reasons for establishing an orphan home are:

- ▸ That God may be glorified, should He be pleased to furnish me with the means, in its being seen that it is not a vain thing to trust in Him; and that the faith of His children may be strengthened.
- ▸ The spiritual welfare of fatherless and motherless children.
- ▸ Their temporal welfare.

That to which my mind has been particularly directed is to establish an orphan home in which destitute fatherless and motherless children may be provided with food and clothing and a scriptural education. Concerning this intended orphan home I would say:

1. It is intended to be in connection with the Scripture Knowledge Institution for Home and Abroad, in so far as it respects the reports, accounts, superintendence, and the principles through which it is conducted. So that, in one sense, it may be considered as a new object of the Institution, yet with the difference, *that only those funds shall be applied to the orphan home that are expressly given for it.* If therefore, any believer would prefer to support either those objects that have been hitherto assisted by the fund of this Institution, or the intended orphan home, it need only be mentioned in order that the money may be applied accordingly.

2. It will only be established if the Lord should provide both the means for it and suitable persons to conduct it. As to the means, I would make the following remarks: The reasons for proposing to enlarge the field are not because we have been rather financially pressed of late. The many gracious answers, however, which the Lord had given us concerning the Institution led Brother C—r and me to give ourselves to prayer, asking Him to supply us with the means to carry on the work as we consider it unscriptural to contract debts. During five days, we prayed several times, both together and separately. After that time, the Lord began to answer our prayers, so that within a few days about 50£. (50 pounds) was given to us. I would further say that the very gracious and tender dealings of God with me in having supplied in answer to prayer for the last five years my own temporal wants without any certain income so that money, provisions, and clothes have been sent to me at times when I was greatly in need and that

not only in small but large quantities. These gifts coming not only from individuals living in the same place with me, but at a considerable distance, also not only from intimate friends, but from individuals whom I have never seen. All this I say has often led me to think, even as long as four years ago, that the Lord had not give me this simple reliance on Him merely for myself, but also for others. Often, when I saw poor neglected children running around the streets at Teignmouth, I said to myself: "May it not be the will of God that I should establish schools for these children, asking Him to give me the means?"

However, it remained only a thought in my mind for two or three years. About two years and six months since I was particularly stirred up afresh to do something for destitute children, by seeing so many of them begging in the streets of Bristol, and coming to our door. It was not, then, left undone on account of want of trust in the Lord, but through an abundance of other things calling for all the time and strength of my Brother Craik and myself. For the Lord had both given faith, and had also shown by the following instance, in addition to very many others, both what He can and what He will do. One morning, while sitting in my room, I thought about the distress of certain brethren, and said to myself: "Oh, that it might please the Lord to give me the means to help these poor brethren!" About an hour later I had 60 pound sent as a present for myself from a brother whom up to this day I have never seen, and who was then and still is residing several thousand miles away. Should not such an experience, together with the promises like that one in John 14:13-14 encourage us to ask with all boldness for ourselves and others both temporal and spiritual blessings?

The Lord, for I cannot but think it was He, again and again brought the thought about these poor children to my mind, till at last it ended in the establishment of *The Scriptural Knowledge Institution for Home and Abroad.* Since its establishment I have had the same thought brought to my mind repeatedly, but especially during the last few weeks to establish an orphan home. My frequent prayer lately has been that if it be of God He will bring it to pass, if not, that He would take all thought of it from me. However, the latter has not been the case, but I have been led more and more to think that it must be of Him. Now, if so, He can influence His people in any part of the world, for I do not look to Bristol, nor England, but to the living God who's gold and silver it is to entrust me and Brother C—r, whom the Lord has made willing to help me in this work with the means. Until we have them, we can do nothing in the way of renting a house, furnishing it, etc. Yet, when once as much as is needed for this has been sent to us, along with proper persons to engage in the work, we do not think it needful to wait until we have the orphan home endowed, or a number of yearly subscribers for it; but we trust to be enabled by the Lord who has taught us to ask for our daily bread, to supply the daily needs of those children whom He may be pleased to put under our care. Any donations will be received at my home. Should any believers have tables, chairs, bedsteads, bedding, dishes, or any kind of household furniture to spare for the furnishing of the home. Also remnants or pieces of calico, linen, flannel, cloth or any materials useful for wearing apparel, or clothes no longer needed will be thankfully received.

Regarding the persons needed for carrying on the work, a matter of no less importance that the procuring of funds, I would observe that we look for them to God himself, as well as for the funds, and that all who may be engaged as masters, matrons, and assistants, according to the size of the Institution, must be known to us as true believers; and moreover, as far as we may be able to judge, must likewise be qualified for the work.

3. At present nothing can be said as to the time when the operations are likely to commence; nor whether the Institution will care for children of both sexes, or be restricted to boys or girls exclusively. Also the age and how long they may continue in it, we wish to be guided in these particulars by the amount of means the Lord may put into our hands and by the number of individuals He may provide for conducting the Institution. If the Lord condescends to use us as instruments, a short printed statement will be issued as soon as something more definite can be said.

4. It has appeared well to us to receive only such destitute children as have been bereaved of both parents.

5. The children are intended, if girls, to be brought up for service; if boys, for a trade; and therefore they will be employed according to their ability and bodily strength in useful occupations, and thus help to maintain themselves. Besides this they are intended to receive a plain education but the chief and special end of the Institution will be to seek with God's

blessing to bring them to the knowledge of the Lord Jesus Christ by instructing them in the Scriptures.

A Testimony Regarding Asking for Funds for the Orphan Home

When praying and asking the Lord about the establishing of a Home for Orphans, I sought His will if it should be done or not. However, in all that time I never asked the Lord for the money or the persons to engage in the work. On December 5th, however, the subject of my prayer all at once became different. I was reading Psalm 81:10 and was with its content: *"Open thy mouth wide and I will fill it."* I thought for a few moments about these words and then was led to apply them to the case of the orphan home. It struck me that I had never asked the Lord for anything concerning it, except to know His will respecting its establishment or not. I then fell on my knees and opened my mouth wide, and without fixing a time when He should answer my petition. I prayed that he would give me a house, i.e., either as a loan, or that someone might be led to pay the rent for one, or that one might be given permanently for this object; furthermore I asked Him for 1000 pounds, and likewise for suitable persons to take care of the children. Besides this, I have been since led to ask the Lord to put it into the hearts of His people to send me articles of furniture for the home, and some clothes for the children. When I was asking the petition I was fully aware what I was doing, i.e., that I was asking for something that I had no natural prospect of obtaining from the brethren whom I know, but which was not too much for the Lord to grant.

Chapter 1

BEGINNING AND EARLY DAYS
OF THE ORPHAN WORK

*"That the trial of your faith, being much more
precious than of gold that perisheth, though it be tried
with fire, might be found unto praise and honour and
glory at the appearing of Jesus Christ."* (1 Peter 1:7)

MR. GEORGE MÜELLER, the founder of the
New Orphan Houses, Ashley Down, Bristol
(institutions that have been for many years
the greatest monuments of modern times to a prayer
answering God), gives in that most valuable and instructive
book, "A Narrative of Some of the Lord's Dealings with
George Müeller," Vol. I., among other reasons for establishing
an Orphan House, the following:

OLD AGE

"Sometimes I found children of God tried in mind by
the prospect of old age, when they might be unable to work
any longer, and therefore were harassed by the fear of having
to go into the poorhouse. If in such a case I pointed out to
them, how their heavenly Father has always helped those
who put their trust in Him, they might not always say that
times have changed; but yet it was evident enough, that God
was not looked upon by them as the *Living* God. My spirit
was often times bowed down by this, and I longed to set
something before the children of God, whereby they might
see, that He does not forsake, even in our day, those who
rely upon Him."

BUSINESS PERSONS

"Another class of persons was brethren in business, who suffered in their souls, and brought guilt on their consciences, by carrying on their business, almost in the same way as unconverted persons do. The competition in trade, the bad times, the over-population of the country, were given as reasons why, if the business were carried on simply according to the Word of God, it could not be expected to do well. Such a brother, perhaps, would express the wish, that he might be differently situated; but very rarely did I see that there was a stand made for God, that there was the holy determination to trust in the living God, and to depend on Him, in order that a good conscience might be maintained. To this class likewise I desired to show, by a visible proof, that God is unchangeably the same."

THE PROFESSIONAL PERSONS

"Then there was another class of persons, individuals who were in professions in which they could not continue with a good conscience, or persons who were in an unscriptural position with reference to spiritual things; but both classes feared, on account of the consequences, to give up the profession in which they could not abide with God, or to leave their position, lest they should be thrown out of employment. My spirit longed to be instrumental in strengthening their faith, by giving them not only instances from the Word of God, of His willingness and ability to help all those who rely upon Him, but to show them by proofs that He is the same in our day. I well knew that the Word of God ought to be enough, and it was, by grace, enough, to me; but still, I considered that I ought to lend a helping hand to my brethren, if by any means, by this visible proof to the unchangeable faithfulness of the Lord, I might strengthen their hands in God; for I remembered what a great blessing my own soul had received through the Lord's dealings with His servant A. H. Francké, who in dependence upon the living God alone, established an immense Orphan House, which I had seen many times with my own eyes."

"I, therefore, judged myself bound to be the servant of the Church of God, in the particular point on which I had obtained mercy: namely, in being able to take God by His Word and to rely upon it. All these exercises of my soul, which resulted from the fact that so many believers with whom I became acquainted were harassed and distressed in mind, or brought guilt on their consciences because of not trusting in the Lord; were used by God to awaken in my heart the desire of setting before the Church at large, and before the world, a proof that He has not in the least changed; and this seemed to me best done by the establishing of an Orphan House. It needed to be something which could be seen, even by the natural eye."

PRIMARY REASON FOR ESTABLISHING THE ORPHAN HOMES

"Now, if I, a poor man, simply by prayer and faith, obtained without asking any individual the means for establishing and carrying on an Orphan House with the Lord's blessing that would be something instrumental in strengthening the faith of the children of God. It would also be a testimony to the consciences of the unconverted of the reality of the things of God. This, then, was the primary reason for establishing the Orphan House.

'I certainly did from my heart desire to be used by God to benefit the bodies and lives of poor children bereaved of both parents, and seek in other respects, with the help of God, to do them good for this life. I also particularly longed to be used by God in getting the dear orphans trained up in the fear of God; however, the first and primary object of the work was and is that God might be magnified by the fact that the orphans under my care are provided with all they need only by prayer and faith. No one being asked by me or my fellow laborers whereby it may be seen, that God *is faithful still, and hears prayer still.*

That I was not mistaken has been abundantly proved since November, 1835, both by the conversion of many sinners who have read the accounts that have been published in connection with this work, and also by the abundance of fruit that has followed in the hearts of the saints. From my inmost soul I desire to be grateful to God by the honor and glory that is due to Him alone, and which I, by His help am enabled to ascribe to Him."

"OPEN THY MOUTH WIDE"
PSALM 81:10B

In the account written by Mr. Müeller dated Jan. 16, 1836, regarding the Orphan House intended to be established in Bristol in connection with the Scriptural Knowledge Institution for Home and Abroad, we read:

PRAYER FOR GOD'S WILL
REGARDING AN ORPHAN HOME

"Lately when the thoughts of establishing an Orphan House in total dependence upon the Lord revived in my mind, I prayed only for the first two weeks that if it were of the Lord He would bring it about, but if not, He would graciously be pleased to take all thoughts about it out of my mind. My uncertainty about knowing the Lord's mind did not arise from questioning whether it would be pleasing in His sight, that there should be a home and scriptural education provided for destitute fatherless and motherless children; but whether it was His will that I should be the instrument of bringing such a work into being, as my hands were already more than filled. My comfort, however, was that if it were His will He would provide not merely the means, but also suitable individuals to take care of the children. In that way, my part of the work would take only a portion of my time when considering the importance of the matter and my many other engagements. The whole of those two weeks I never asked the Lord for money or for persons to engage in the work."

"On December 5th, however, the subject of my prayer all at once became different. I was reading Psalm 81, and was particularly struck more than at any time before with verse 10: "Open thy mouth wide, and I will fill it." I thought a few moments about these words, and then was led to apply them to the case of the Orphan House. It struck me that I had never asked the Lord for anything concerning it, except to know His will, regarding its being established or not; and I then fell on my knees and opened my mouth wide, asking Him for much. I asked in submission to His will, and without fixing a time when He should answer my petition. I prayed that He would give me a house, i.e., either as a loan, or that someone might be led to pay the rent for one, or that one might be given permanently for this object, Further, I asked Him for £1000; and likewise for suitable individuals to take care of the children. Besides this, I have been since led to ask the Lord, to put into the hearts of His people to send me articles of furniture for the house, and some clothes for the children. When I was asking the petition, I was fully aware what I was doing, I.e., that I was asking for something that I had no natural prospect of obtaining from the brethren whom I know, but which was not too much for the Lord to grant."

"December 10, 1835. This morning I received a letter, in which a brother and sister wrote thus: 'We propose to offer ourselves for the service of the intended Orphan House if you think us qualified for it. We plan also to give up all the furniture, and other comforts that the Lord has given us for its use; and to do this without receiving any salary whatever; believing that if it be the will of the Lord to employ us He will supply all our needs, and comforts."

"December 13, 1835. A brother was influenced this day to give 4s. Per week, or £10 8s. Yearly, as long as the Lord gives the means. 8s. was given by him every two weeks. To-day a brother and sister offered themselves, with all their furniture, and all the provisions which they have in the house, if they can be usefully employed in the concerns of the Orphan House."

A GREAT ENCOURAGEMENT

"December 17. I was rather cast down last evening and this morning about the matter, questioning whether I ought to be engaged in this way, and was led to ask the Lord to give me some further encouragement. Soon after were sent by a brother two pieces of printed cloth, the one seven and the other 23¾ yards, 6¾ yards of calico, four pieces of lining, about four yards altogether, a sheet, and a yard measure. This evening another brother brought a clothes horse, three frocks, four pinafores, six handkerchiefs, three counterpanes, one blanket, two pewter salt cellars, six tin cups, and six metal tea spoons; he also brought 3s. 6d. given to him by three different individuals. At the same time he told me that it had been put into the heart of an individual to send to-morrow £100."

ONE THOUSAND POUNDS

"June 15, 1837. Today I gave myself once more earnestly to prayer respecting the remainder of the £1000. This evening £5 was given, so that now the whole sum is made up. To the glory of the Lord, whose I am, and whom I serve, I would state again that every shilling of this money, and all the articles of clothing and furniture that have been mentioned in the foregoing pages have been given to me without one single individual having been asked by me for anything."

ORPHANS FOR THE BUILDING

In a third statement, containing the announcement of the opening of the Orphan House for destitute female children, and a proposal for the establishment of an Infant Orphan House, which was sent to the press on May 18, 1836, Mr. Müeller wrote: "So far as I remember, I brought even the most minute circumstances concerning the Orphan House before the Lord in my petitions, being conscious of my own weakness and ignorance. There was, however, one point I never had prayed about, namely that the Lord would send children; for I naturally took it for granted that there would be plenty of applications. The nearer, however, the day came which had been appointed for receiving applications, the more I had a secret consciousness that the Lord might disappoint my natural expectations, and show me that I could not prosper in one single thing without Him.

The appointed time came and not even one application was made. I had before this been repeatedly tried in mind whether I might have against the Lord's mind been engaged in the work. This circumstance now led me to lie low before my God in prayer the whole of the evening of February 3. I examined my heart once more as to all the motives concerning it; and being able to say that His glory was my chief aim so it might be seen that it is not a vain thing to trust in the living God. And that my second aim was the spiritual welfare of the orphan children, and the third their bodily welfare. Still continuing in prayer, I was at last brought to the state that I could say from my heart that I would rejoice in God being glorified in this matter even if He might bring it to nothing. But it still seemed to me to be more tending to the glory of God to establish and prosper the Orphan House; I could then ask Him heartily to send applications. I enjoyed now a peaceful state of heart concerning the subject, and was also more assured than ever that God would establish it. The very next day, February 4, the first application was made, and since then 42 more have been made."

"JUST FOR TODAY"

Later on, when there were nearly 100 persons to be maintained, and the funds were reduced to about £20, Mr. Müeller writes:

"July 22, 1838. This evening I was walking in our little garden and meditating on Hebrews 13:8, *"Jesus Christ the same yesterday, and today, and for ever."* While meditating on His unchangeable love, power, wisdom, etc., and turning it all as I went into prayer respecting myself, I likewise applied His unchangeable love, power, and wisdom to both my present spiritual and temporal circumstances and all at once the present need of the Orphan House was brought to my mind. Immediately I was led to say to myself, Jesus in His love and power has hitherto supplied me with what I have needed for the Orphans, and in the same unchangeable love and power He will provide me with what I may need for the future. A flow of joy came into my soul as I realized the unchangeableness of our adorable Lord. About one minute later, a letter was brought to me with £20 enclosed. In it was written: "Please apply the amount of the enclosed money to the furtherance of the objects of your Scriptural Knowledge Society, your Orphan Establishment, or in the work and cause of our Master in any way that He himself may point out to you. It is not a great sum, but it is a sufficient provision for the exigency of today; and it is for today›s exigencies that the Lord provides. Tomorrow, as it brings its demands, will find its supply, etc."

"Of this £20 I took £10 for the Orphan fund, and £10 for the other objects and thereby was enabled to meet the expenses of about £34 that in connection with the Orphan Houses came upon me within four days afterwards, and which I knew beforehand would come."

WAITING FOR HELP

"November 21, 1838. Never were we so reduced in funds as today. There was not a single halfpenny in hand between the matrons of the three houses. Nevertheless there was a good dinner, and by managing so as to help one another with bread, etc., there was a prospect of getting over this day also; but not one of the houses had the prospect of being able to take in bread for further need. When I left the brothers and sisters at one o'clock, after prayer, I told them that we must wait for help, and see how the Lord would deliver us this time. I was sure of help, but we were indeed in dire need. When I came to Kingsdown, I felt that I needed more exercise as it was very cold; therefore, I did not go the nearest way home, but around by Clarence Place. About twenty yards from my house, I met a brother who walked along with me, and after a little conversation gave me £10 to be handed over to the deacons towards providing the poor saints with coals, blankets and warm clothing; also £5 for the Orphans, and £5 for the other objects of the Scriptural Knowledge Institution. The brother had called twice while I was gone to the Orphan Houses, and had I been one half minute later, I would have missed him. But the Lord knew our need, and therefore allowed me to meet him. I sent off the £5 immediately to the matrons."

BEYOND DISAPPOINTMENT

"September 21, 1840, Monday. By what was in hand for the Orphans, and by what had come in yesterday, the need of today is more than supplied, as there is enough for to- morrow also. Today a brother from the neighborhood of London gave me £10, to be laid out as it might be most needed. As we have been praying many days for the School, Bible, and Missionary Funds, I took it all for them. This brother knew nothing about our work, when he came three days prior to Bristol. Thus the Lord, to show His continued care over us, raises up new helpers. They that trust in the Lord shall never be confounded! Some who helped for a while may fall asleep in Jesus; others may grow cold in the service of the Lord; others may be as desirous as ever to help, but have no longer the means; others may have both a willing heart to help, and have also the means, but may see it the Lord's will is to lay them out in another way.

Therefore, from one cause or another, if were we to lean upon man, we would surely be confounded; but, in leaning upon the living God alone, we are *beyond disappointment and beyond* being forsaken because of death or want of means or want of love or because of the claims of other work. How precious to have learned in any measure to stand with God alone in the world, and yet to be happy, and to know that surely no good thing shall be withheld from us while we walk uprightly!"

A GREAT SINNER CONVERTED

In his "Review of the Year 1841," Mr. Müeller writes:

"During this year I was informed about the conversion of one of the very greatest sinners that I ever heard of in all my service for the Lord. Repeatedly I fell on my knees with his wife, and asked the Lord for his conversion, when she came to me in the deepest distress of soul on account of the most barbarous and cruel treatment that she received from him in his bitter enmity against her for the Lord's sake because he could not provoke her to be in a passion, and she would not strike him, and the like. At the time when it was at its worst I pleaded especially on his behalf the promise in Matthew 18:19: '*Again I say unto you, that if two of you shall agree on earth as touching anything that they shall ask, it shall be done for them of my father which is in heaven.*' And now this awful persecutor is converted."

PRAYER FOR THE SPIRITUAL BLESSING AMONG THE SAINTS

"On May 25th, 1845, I began to ask the Lord for greater real spiritual prosperity for the saints among whom I labor in Bristol than there had ever yet been among them. Now I have to record to the praise of the Lord that truly He has answered this request; for considering all things, at no period has there been more manifestation of grace and truth, and spiritual power among us than there is now while I am writing this for the press. Not that we have attained to what we might; we are far, very far from it; but the Lord has been very, very good to us, and we have most abundant cause for thanksgiving."

WITHHOLDING THE REPORT

"December 9, 1841. Today there came in for the Orphans by the sale of stockings 10s. 10d. We are now brought to the close of the sixth year of this part of the work, and having only in hand the money which has been put by for the rent; but during the whole of this year we have been supplied with all that was needed.

"During the last three years we had closed the accounts on this day, and a few days later we had some public meetings, at which, for the benefit of the hearers we stated how the Lord had dealt with us during the year, and the substance of what had been stated at these meetings was afterwards printed for the benefit of the Church at large.

'This time, however, it appeared to us better to delay for a while both the public meetings and the publishing of the Report. Through grace we had learned to lean upon the Lord only, being assured that if we were never to speak or write one single word more about this work we would be supplied with means as long as He would enable us to depend on Him alone. But while we neither had those public meetings for the purpose of exposing our necessity, nor had the account of the Lord's dealings with us published for the sake of working upon the feelings of the readers to give us money, it might have appeared to some that in making known our circumstances we did so for those motives and not to benefit the saint by observing what God had done for us. What better proof, therefore, could we give of our depending upon the living God alone, and not upon public meetings or printed Reports, than when in the midst of our deep poverty instead of being glad for the time to have come when we could make known our circumstances, we still went on quietly for some time longer, without saying anything. We therefore determined, as we sought and still seek in this work to act for the profit of the saints generally, to delay both the public meetings and the Report for a few months. In the natural we would have been as glad as anyone to have exposed our poverty at that time; but spiritually we were unable to delight even then in the prospect of the increased benefit that might be derived by the Church at large from our acting as we did."

THE GREATEST NEED

"December 18, Saturday morning. There is now the greatest need, and only 4d. in hand, which I found in the box at my house; yet I fully believe the Lord will supply us this day also with all that is required. Pause a few moments, dear reader! Observe two things. We acted for God in delaying the public meetings and the publishing of the Report; but God's way leads always into trial so far as sight and sense are concerned.

Nature will always be tried in God's ways. The Lord was saying by this poverty, 'I will now see whether you truly lean upon me, and whether you truly look to me.' Of all the seasons that I had ever passed through since I had been living in this way, up to that time, I never knew any period in which my faith was tried so sharply, as during the four months from December 12, 1841, to April 12, 1842. But observe further: We might even now have altered our minds with respect to the public meetings and publishing the Report; for no one knew our determination, at this time concerning the point. Nay, on the contrary, we knew with what delight very many children of God were looking forward to receive further accounts. But the Lord kept us steadfast to the conclusion at which we had arrived under His guidance."

"HE ABIDETH FAITHFUL"
(2 TIMOTHY 2:13)

Under the date January 25, 1842, Mr. Müeller writes: "Perhaps, dear reader, you have said in your heart before you have read thus far: 'How would it be if the funds for the Orphans were reduced to nothing, and those who are engaged in the work had nothing of their own to give, and a meal time were to come, and you had no food for the children? Thus indeed it may be, for our hearts are desperately wicked. If ever we would be so left to ourselves that either we depend no more upon the living God, or that *we regard iniquity in our hearts,*' then such a state of things we have reason to believe, would occur. But so long as we shall be enabled to trust in the living God, and so long as, though falling short in every way of what we might be, and ought to be, we are at least kept from living in sin, such a state of things cannot occur. Therefore, dear reader, if you yourself walk with God, and if, on that account, His glory is dear to you, I affectionately and earnestly entreat you to beseech Him to uphold us. For how awful would be the disgrace brought upon His holy name if we, who have so publicly made our boast in Him, and have spoken well of Him, should be left to disgrace Him either by unbelief in the hour of trial, or by a life of sin in other respects."

DELAYED BUT SURE

"March 9, 1842. At a time of the greatest need, both with regard to the Day Schools and the Orphans, so much so that we could not have gone on any longer without help, I received this day £10 from a brother who lives near Dublin. The money was divided between the Day Schools and the Orphan Houses. The following little circumstance is to be noticed respecting this donation: As our need was so great, and my soul was, through grace, truly waiting upon the Lord, I looked out for supplies in the course of this morning. The post, however, was out, and no supplies had come. This did not in the least discourage me. I said to myself, the Lord can send means without the post, or even now, though the post is out by this very delivery of letters He may have sent means though the money is not yet in my hands. It was not long after I had thus spoken to myself, when, according to my hope in God, we were helped; for the brother who sent us the £10, had this time directed his letter to the Boys' Orphan House, when it was sent to me."

LIKE AS A FATHER

"March 17. From the 12th to the 16th had come in £4 5s. 11½d. for the Orphans. This morning our poverty, which now has lasted more or less for several months, had become exceedingly great. I left my house a few minutes after seven to go to the Orphan Houses, to see whether there was money enough to take in the milk, which is brought about eight o'clock. On my way it was especially my request that the Lord would be pleased to pity us, even as a father pitieth his children, and that He would not lay more upon us than He would enable us to bear, I especially asked Him if He would now be pleased to refresh our hearts by sending us help. I likewise reminded Him of the consequences that would result, both in reference to believers and unbelievers if we should have to give up the work because of want of means, and that He therefore would not permit of it coming to that.

I moreover again confessed before the Lord that I deserved not that He should continue to use me in this work any longer. While I was thus in prayer, about two minutes' walk from the Orphan Houses, I met a brother who was going at this early hour to his business. After having exchanged a few words with him, I went on; but he presently ran after me, and gave me £1 for the Orphans. Thus the Lord speedily answered my prayer. Truly, it is worth being poor and greatly tried in faith, for the sake of having day by day such precious proofs of the loving interest which our kind Father takes in everything that concerns us. And how should our Father do otherwise? He that has given us the greatest possible proof of His love which He could have done, in giving us His own Son, surely He will with Him also freely give us all things."

TRUST IN THE LORD
BETTER THAN MAN'S PROMISES

"May 6, 1845. About six weeks ago intimation was kindly given by a brother that he expected a certain considerable sum of money, and that, if he obtained it, a certain portion of it should be given to the Lord, so that £100 of it should be used for the work in my hands, and the other part for Brother Craik's and my own personal expenses. However, day after day passed away, and the money did not come. I did not trust in this money, yet, as during all this time, with scarcely any exception, we were more or less needy, I thought again and again about this brother's promise; though I did not, by the grace of God, trust in the brother who had made it, but in the Lord. Thus week after week passed away, and the money did not come. Now this morning it came to my mind, that such promises ought to be valued, in a certain sense, as nothing, and that the mind ought never for a moment be directed to them, but to the living God, and to the living God only. I saw that such promises ought not to be of the value of one farthing, so far as it regards thinking about them for help. I therefore asked the Lord, when, as usual, I was praying with my beloved wife about the work in my hands that He would be pleased to take this whole matter about that promise completely out of my mind, and to help me not to value it in the least but to treat it as it was not worth one farthing, but to keep my eye directed only upon Him. I was enabled to do so. We had not yet finished praying when I received the following letter:

> May 5, 1845
> Beloved Brother,
>
> Are your bankers still Messrs. Stuckey and Co. of Bristol, and are their bankers still Messrs. Robarts and Co. of London?
>
> Please instruct me on this; and if the case should be so, please regard this as a letter of advice that £70 are paid to Messrs. Robarts and Co., for Messrs. Stuckey and Co., for you. Apply this sum as the Lord may give you wisdom. I shall not send to Robarts and Co. until I hear from you.
>
> Ever affectionately yours,

"Thus the Lord rewarded at once this determination to endeavor not to look in the least to that promise from a brother, but only to Him. But this was not all. About two o'clock this afternoon I received from the brother, who had more than forty days ago, made that promise, £166 18s, as he this day received the money, on the strength of which he had made that promise. Of this sum £100 are to be used for the work in my hands, and the remainder for Brother Craik's and my own personal expenses."

UNDER THE DATE 1842
MR. MÜELLER WRITES:

"I desire that all the children of God, who may read these details, may thereby be lead to increased and more simple confidence in God for everything which they may need under any circumstances, and that these many answers to prayer may encourage them to pray, particularly as it regards the conversion of their friends and relatives, their own progress in grace and knowledge, the state of the saints whom they may know personally, the state of the Church of God at large, and the success of the preaching of the Gospel. I especially affectionately warn them against being led away by the devices of Satan to think that these things are peculiar to me, and cannot be enjoyed by all the children of God. For though, as has been stated before, every believer is not called upon to establish Orphan Houses, Charity Schools, etc., and trust in the Lord for means. Yet all believers are called upon in the simple confidence of faith to cast all their burdens upon Him, to trust in Him for everything, and not only to make everything a subject of prayer, but to expect answers to their petitions which they have asked according to His will, and in the name of the Lord Jesus.

"Think not, dear reader, that I have the gift of faith, that is, that gift of which I read in 1 Corinthians 12:9, and which is mentioned along with 'the gifts of healing,' 'the working of miracles,' 'prophecy,' and because of that I am able to trust in the Lord. It is true that the faith, which I am enabled to exercise, is altogether God's own gift; it is true that He alone supports it, and that He alone can increase it; it is true that, moment by moment, I depend upon Him for it, and that if I were only one moment left to myself, my faith would utterly fail; but it is not true that my faith is that gift of faith which is spoken of in 1 Corinthians 12:9 for the following reasons:

1. The faith which I am enabled to exercise with reference to the Orphan Houses and my own temporal necessities, is not that 'faith' of which it is said in 1 Corinthians 12:2 (evidently in allusion to the faith spoken of in 1 Corinthians 12:9), *'Though I have all faith, so that I could remove mountains, and have not charity (love), I am nothing'*; but it is the self-same faith which is found in every believer and the growth of which I am most sensible of to myself; for little by little it has been increasing for the last sixty-nine years.

2. This faith which is exercised respecting the Orphan Houses and my own temporal necessities, shows itself in the same measure, for instance concerning the following points: I have never been permitted to doubt during the last sixty-nine years that my sins are forgiven, that I am a child of God, that I am beloved of God, and that I shall be finally Saved. Why? Because I am enabled by the grace of God to exercise faith upon the Word of God, and believe what God says in those passages that settle these matters (1 John 1:1-2, Galatians 3:26, Acts 10:43, Romans 10:9-10, John 3:16, etc.). Further, when sometimes all has been dark, exceedingly dark with reference to my service among the saints, judging from natural appearances when I should have been overwhelmed indeed in grief and despair, if I had looked at things by their outward appearance, I would at such times sought to encourage myself in God by laying hold in faith on His mighty power, His unchangeable love, and His infinite wisdom. At that time I have said to myself: God is able and willing to deliver me, if it be good for me; for it is written: *"He that spared not His own Son, but delivered Him up for us all, how shall He not with Him also freely give us all things?"* Romans 8:32. This being believed by me through grace, kept my soul in peace.

'Furthermore, when in connection with the Orphan Houses, Day Schools, etc., trials have come upon me that were far heavier than the want of means when lying reports were spread that the Orphans had not enough to eat, or that they were cruelly treated in other respects, and the like. Or when other trials, still greater, but which I cannot mention, have befallen me in connection with this work. One time in particular when I was nearly a thousand miles absent from Bristol, and had to remain absent week after week: at such times my soul was stayed upon God; I believed His Word of promise which was applicable to such cases; I poured out my soul before God, and arose from my knees in peace, because the trouble that was in the soul was in believing prayer cast upon God, and thus I was kept in peace, though I saw it to be the will of God to remain far away from the work. Further still, when I needed houses, fellow laborers, masters and mistresses for the Orphans or for the Day Schools, I have been enabled to look for all to the Lord and trust in Him for help.

'Dear reader, I may seem to boast; but, by the grace of God, I do not boast in thus speaking. From my inmost soul I do ascribe it to God alone that He has enabled me to trust in Him, and that hitherto He has not allowed my confidence in Him to fail. But I thought it needful to make these remarks, lest anyone should think that my depending upon God was a particular gift given to me, which other saints have no right to look for; or lest it should be thought that my depending upon Him had only to do with the obtaining of *money* by prayer and faith. By the grace of God I desire that my faith in God should extend towards *everything*, the smallest of my own temporal and spiritual concerns, and the smallest of the temporal and spiritual concerns of my family, towards the saints among whom I labor, the Church at large, and everything that has to do with the temporal and spiritual prosperity of the Scriptural Knowledge Institution, etc.

'Dear reader, do not think that I have attained in faith (and how much less in other aspects) to that degree to which I might and ought to attain; but thank God for the faith which He has given me, and ask Him to uphold and increase it. And lastly, once more, let not Satan deceive you in making you think that you could not have the same faith because it is only for persons who are situated as I am.

▸ When I lose such a thing as a key, I ask the Lord to direct me to it.

▸ I look for an answer to my prayer; when a person with whom I have made an appointment does not come according to the fixed time, and I begin to be inconvenienced by it, I ask the Lord to be pleased to hasten him to me.

▸ I look for an answer; when I do not understand a passage of the Word of God, I lift up my heart to the Lord, that He would be pleased, by His Holy Spirit to instruct me, and I expect to be taught, though I do not fix the time when, and the manner how it should be.

▸ When I am going to minister in the Word, I seek help from the Lord, and while I, in the consciousness of natural inability as well as utter unworthiness begin this His service, I am not cast down, but of good cheer, because I look for His assistance, and believe that He, for His dear Son's sake will help me.

▸ And thus in other of my temporal and spiritual concerns I pray to the Lord, and expect an answer to my requests; and may not you do the same, dear believing reader?

Oh! I beseech you, do not think me as an extraordinary believer having privileges above other of God's dear children, which they cannot have; nor look on my way of acting as something that would not do for other believers. Make yourself fast in faith in trials! Do but stand still in the hour of trial, and you will see the help of God, if you trust in Him. But there is so often a forsaking the ways of the Lord in the hour of trial, and thus the food of faith the means whereby our faith may be increased, is lost."

HOW CAN A BELIEVER HAVE HIS FAITH STRENGTHENED?

"This leads me to the following important point. You ask, how may I, a true believer, have my faith strengthened? The answer is this:

Every good gift and every perfect gift is from above, and cometh down from the Father of lights, with whom is no variableness, neither shadow of turning." James 1:17. As the increase of faith is a good gift, it must come from God, and therefore He ought to be asked for this blessing"

"The following means, however, ought to be used:

The careful reading of the Word of God combined with meditation on it. Through reading of the Word of God, and especially through meditation on the Word of God, the believer becomes more and more acquainted with the nature and character of God, and thus sees more and more, besides His holiness and justice, what a kind, loving, gracious, merciful, mighty, wise, and faithful Being He is, and, therefore, in poverty, affliction of body, bereavement in his family, difficulty in his service, want of a situation or employment, he will rest upon the ability of God to help him. Because he has not only learned from His Word that He is of almighty power and infinite wisdom, but he has also seen instance upon instance in the Holy Scriptures in which His almighty power and infinite wisdom have been actually exercised in helping and delivering His people.

'He will also rest upon the willingness of God to help him, because he has not only learned from the Scriptures what a kind, good, merciful, gracious, and faithful being God is, but because he has also seen in the Word of God how in a great variety of instances He has proved himself to be so. And in the consideration of this, if God has become known to us through prayer and meditation on His own Word it will lead us, in general at least, with a measure of confidence to rely upon Him: and thus the reading of the Word of God, together with meditation on it, will be one special means to strengthen our faith."

HOW DOES THE BELIEVER GROW IN THE GRACE OF THE SPIRIT?

"As with reference to the growth of every grace of the Spirit, it is of the utmost importance that we seek to maintain an upright heart and a good conscience, and therefore, do not knowingly and habitually indulge in those things that are contrary to the mind of God. It is particularly the case with reference to the growth in faith. How can I possibly continue to act faith upon God, concerning anything, if I am habitually grieving Him, and seek to detract from the glory and honor of Him in whom I profess to trust, and upon whom I profess to depend? All my confidence towards God, all my leaning upon Him in the hour of trial will be gone, if I have a guilty conscience, and do not seek to put away this guilty conscience, but still continue to do the things which are contrary to the mind of God.

'And if, in any particular instance, I cannot trust in God, because of the guilty conscience, then my faith is weakened by that instance of distrust; for faith with every fresh trial of it either increases by trusting God, and thus getting help, or it decreases by not trusting Him; and then there is less and less power of looking simply and directly to Him, and a habit of self-dependence is begotten or encouraged. One or the other of these will always be the case in each particular instance. Either we trust in God, and in that case we neither trust in ourselves, nor in our fellow-men, nor in circumstances, nor in anything besides; or we *Do* trust in one or more of these, and in that case do NOT trust in God."

HOW DOES THE BELIEVER GROW IN FAITH DURING TRIALS?

3. 'If we, indeed, desire our faith to be strengthened, we should not shrink from opportunities where our faith may be tried, and, therefore, through the trial, be strengthened. In our natural state we dislike dealing with God alone. Through our natural alienation from God we shrink from Him, and from eternal realities. This cleaves to us more or less, even after our regeneration. Hence it is, that more or less, even as believers, we have the same shrinking from standing with God alone, from depending upon Him alone, from looking to Him alone: and yet this is the very position in which we ought to be if we wish our faith to be strengthened. The more I am in a position to be tried in faith with reference to my body, my family, my service for the Lord, my business, etc., the more I shall have opportunity of seeing God's help and deliverance; and every fresh instance, in which He helps and delivers me, will tend towards the increase of my faith. On this account, therefore, the believer should not shrink from situations, positions, circumstances, in which his faith may be tried; but should cheerfully embrace them as opportunities where he may see the hand of God stretched out on his behalf, to help and deliver him, and whereby he may thus have his faith strengthened."

LEARN TO LET GOD WORK IN YOU DURING A TRIAL OF YOUR FAITH

4. "The last important point for the strengthening of our faith is, that we let God work for us when the hour of the trial of our faith comes, and do not work a deliverance of our own. Wherever God has given faith, it is given among other reasons, for the very purpose of being tried. Yes, however weak our faith may be, God will try it; only with this restriction, that as in every way, He leads on gently, gradually, patiently, so also with reference to the trial of our faith. At first our faith will be tried very little in comparison with what it may be afterwards; for God never lays more upon us that He is willing to enable us to bear. Now when the trial of faith comes, we are naturally inclined to distrust God, and to trust rather in ourselves, or in our friends, or in circumstances.

'We would rather work a deliverance of our own somehow or other, than simply look to God and wait for His help. But if we do not patiently wait for God's help, if we work a deliverance of our own, then at the next trial of our faith it will be the same again, we will be inclined again to deliver ourselves; and thus with every fresh instance of that kind, our faith will decrease; while on the contrary if we were we to stand still in order to see the salvation of God, to see His hand stretched out on our behalf, trusting in Him alone, then our faith would be increased, and with every fresh case in which the hand of God is stretched out on our behalf in the hour of the trial of our faith, our faith would be increased yet more."

SPEND MUCH TIME WITH GOD TO STRENGTHEN YOUR FAITH

"If the believer, therefore, wants to have his faith strengthened, he must especially, give time to God, who tries his faith in order to prove to His child, in the end how willing He is to help and deliver him the moment it is good for him."

EXAMPLES OF SEVERE TRIALS

"In the early years of the Institution Mr. Müeller and his fellow laborers had to endure many severe trials of faith, as some of these instances show. Mr. Müeller when writing of this period says:

'Though now, July of 1845, for about seven years our funds have been so exhausted, that it has been a rare case that there have been means in hand to meet the necessities of more than 100 persons for three days in a row, yet, I have been only once been tried in spirit, and that was on September 18, 1838, when for the first time the Lord seemed not to regard our prayer. But when He did send help at that time, and I saw that it was only for the trial of our faith, and not because He had forsaken the work that we were brought so low, my soul was so strengthened and encouraged, that I have been allowed to distrust the Lord, but have not been even cast down when in the deepest poverty since that time."

A GIFT OF £12

"Aug. 20, 1838. The £5 which I had received on the 18th had been given for house-keeping, so that today I was again penniless. But my eyes were up to the Lord. I gave myself to prayer this morning, knowing that I should want again this week at least £13, if not above £20. Today I received £12 in answer to prayer from a lady who is staying at Clifton, whom I had never seen before. Adorable Lord, grant that this may be a fresh encouragement to me!"

A SOLEMN CRISIS

Regarding one of the sharpest times of trial Mr. Müeller writes:

"September 10, 1838. Monday morning. Neither Saturday nor yesterday had any money come in. It appeared to me now needful to take some steps on account of our need, for example, go to the Orphan Houses and call the brethren and sisters together, (who, except brother T----, had never been informed about the state of the funds), state the case to them, see how much money was needed for the present, tell them that amidst all this trial of faith I still believed that God would help, and to pray with them. Especially, also, I meant to go for the sake of telling them that no more articles must be purchased than we have the means to pay for, but to let there be nothing lacking in any way to the children as it regards nourishing food and needful clothing; for I would rather at once send them away than that they should lack. I meant to go for the sake also of seeing whether there were still articles remaining which had been sent for the purpose of being sold, or whether there were any articles really needless, that we might turn them into money. I felt that the matter was now come to a solemn crisis.

About half-past nine a sixpence came in, which had been put anonymously into the box at Gideon Chapel. This money seemed to me like an earnest, that God would have compassion and send more. About ten, after I had returned from Brother Craik's, to whom I had unbosomed my heart again, while once more in prayer for help, a sister called who gave two sovereigns to my wife for the Orphans, stating that she had felt herself stirred up to come and that she had delayed coming already too long. A few minutes after, when I went into the room where she was, she gave me two sovereigns more, and all this without knowing the least about our need. Thus the Lord most mercifully has sent us a little help, to the great encouragement of my faith. A few minutes after I was called on for money from the Infant Orphan House, to which I sent £2, and £1 0s. 6d. to the Boys' Orphan House, and £1 to the Girls' Orphan House."

A PRECIOUS DELIVERANCE

"September 17, 1838. The trial still continues. It is now more and more trying, even to faith, as each day comes. Truly, the Lord has wise purposes in allowing us to call so long upon Him for help. But I am sure God will send help, if we can but wait. One of the laborers d had a little money come in of which he gave 12s. 6d; another laborer gave 11s. 8d, being all the money she had left; this, with 17s. 6d., which partly had come in, and partly was in hand, enabled us to pay what needed to be paid, and to purchase provisions, so that nothing yet, in any way, has been lacking. This evening I was rather tired especially in the long delay of larger sums coming; but being led to go to the Scriptures for comfort, my soul was greatly refreshed, and my faith again strengthened by Psalm 34, so that I went very cheerfully to meet with my dear fellow laborers for prayer. I read them the Psalm, and sought to cheer their hearts through the precious promises contained in it."

"September 18. Brother T. had 25s. in hand, and I had

3s. This £1 8s. enabled us to buy the meat and bread, which was needed; a little tea for one of the houses, and milk for all; no more than this is needed. Thus the Lord has provided not only for this day; for there is now bread for two days in hand. Now, however, we are come to an extremity. The funds are exhausted. The laborers, who had a little money, have given as long as they had any left. Now observe how the Lord helped us! A lady from the neighborhood of London, who brought a parcel with money from her daughter, arrived four or five days prior in Bristol and took lodgings next door to the Boys' Orphan House. This afternoon she kindly brought me the money, amounting to £3 2s. 6d. We had been reduced so low as to be on the point of selling those things which could be spared; but this morning I had asked the Lord, if it might be, to prevent the necessity, of our doing so. That the money had been so near the Orphan Houses for several days without being given, is a plain proof that it was from the beginning in the heart of God to help us; but because He delights in the prayers of His children, He had allowed us to pray so long to try our faith, and to make the answer so much the sweeter. It is indeed a precious deliverance. I burst out into loud praises and thanks the first moment I was alone, after I had received the money. I met with my fellow laborers again this evening for prayer and praise; their hearts were not a little cheered. This money was this evening divided, and will comfortably provide for all that will be needed tomorrow."

Chapter 2

THE NEW ORPHAN HOUSES AT ASHLEY DOWN

A COMPLAINT having been received from a gentleman in October, 1845, that some of the inhabitants of Wilson Street were inconvenienced by the Orphan Houses being in that street, Mr. Müeller ultimately decided for that and other reasons, after much prayerful meditation, to build an Orphan House elsewhere to accommodate 300 children, and commenced to ask the Lord for means for so doing:

"January 31, 1846. It is now 89 days since I have been daily waiting upon God about the building of an Orphan House. The time seems to me now near when the Lord will give us a piece of ground, and I told the brothers and sisters so this evening, after our usual Saturday evening prayer meeting at the Orphan Houses.

"February 1. A poor widow sent 10s today.

"February 2. Today I heard of suitable and cheap land on Ashley Down.

"February 3. Saw the land. It is the most desirable of all I have seen. There was anonymously put in an Orphan box at my house, a sovereign in a piece of paper on which was written, 'The New Orphan House.'

"February 4. This evening I called on the owner of the land on Ashley Down about which I had heard on the 2nd of February, but he was not at home. As I had been informed that I should find him at his house of business, I went there, but did not find him there either as he had just before left. I might have called again at his residence at a later hour having been informed by one of the servants that he would be sure to be at home about eight o'clock; but I did not do so, judging that there was the hand of God in my not finding him at either place: and I judged it best not to force the matter, but to 'let patience have her perfect work.'

"February 5. I saw the owner of the land this morning. He told me that he awoke at three o'clock this morning and could not sleep again till five. While he was thus lying awake his mind was all the time occupied about the piece of land regarding the inquiry that had been made of him for the building of an Orphan House. At my request he determined that if I should apply for it, he would not only let me have it, but for £120 per acre, instead of £200; the price which he had previously asked for it. How good is the Lord! The agreement was made this morning, and I purchased a field of nearly seven acres, at £120 per acre.

"Observe the hand of God in my not finding the owner at home last evening! The Lord meant to speak to His servant first about this matter, during a sleepless night, and to lead him to fully decide before I had seen him."

"BECAUSE OF HIS IMPORTUNITY"

"November 19, 1846. I am now led more and more to importune the Lord to send me the means, which are required in order that I may be able to commence the building. (1) Because it has been for some time publicly stated in print, that I remember it is not without grounds that some of the inhabitants of Wilson Street consider themselves inconvenienced by the Orphan Houses being in that street. Therefore, I long to be able to remove the Orphans from there as soon as possible. (2) I become more and more convinced that it would be greatly for the benefit of the children, both physically and morally, with God's blessing to be in such a position as they are intended to occupy when the New Orphan House shall have been built. (3) And because the number of very poor and destitute Orphans that are waiting for admission is so great, and there are constantly fresh applications being made. Now while by God's grace I would not wish the building to be begun one single day sooner than is His will; and while I firmly believe that He will give me in His own time, every shilling that I need I also know that He delights in being earnestly asked and that He takes pleasure in the continuance of prayer and in my importuning Him, which so clearly is to be seen from the parable of the widow and the unjust judge, Luke 18:1-8. For these reasons I gave myself again particularly to prayer last evening that the Lord would send further means. I was also especially led to do so because there had come in comparatively little since the 29th of last month.

'This morning between five and six o'clock I prayed again, among other things, about the Building Fund, and then had a long season for the reading of the Word of God. In the course of my reading I came to Mark 11:24, *'What things soever ye desire, when ye pray, believe that ye receive them, and ye shall have them.'* The importance of the truth contained in this portion I have often felt and spoken about; but this morning I felt it again most positively, and applying it to the New Orphan House, I said to the Lord: 'Lord I believe that Thou wilt give me all I need for this work. I am sure that I shall have all, because I believe that I receive in answer to my prayer.' Thus, with a heart full of peace concerning this work, I went on to the other part of the chapter, and to the next chapter.

'After family prayer I again had my usual season for prayer with regard to all the many parts of the work, and the various necessities thereof. I asked blessings upon my fellow-laborers, upon the circulation of Bibles and Tracts, and upon the precious souls in the Adult School, the Sunday

Schools, the Six Day Schools, and the four Orphan Houses. Amidst all the many things I again made my requests about means for the Building.

'And now observe: About five minutes, after I had risen from my knees, there was given to me a registered letter containing a check for £300, of which £280 are for the Building Fund, £10 for my own personal expenses, and £10 for Brother Craik. The Lord's holy name be praised for this precious encouragement, by which the Building Fund is now increased to more than six thousand pounds."

MR. MÜELLER'S FIRST ORPHAN HOUSE

"January 25, 1847. The season of the year is now approaching, when building may be begun. Therefore with increased earnestness I have given myself unto prayer, importuning the Lord that He would be pleased to appear on our behalf, and speedily send the remainder of the amount which is required, and I have increasingly, of late, felt that the time is drawing near, when the Lord will give me all that which is requisite for commencing the building. All the various arguments which I have often brought before God, I brought also again this morning before Him. It is now 14 months and 3 weeks since day by day I have uttered my petitions to God on behalf of this work. I rose from my knees this morning in full confidence, not only that God could but also would send the means, and soon. Never, during all these 14 months and 3 weeks, have I had the least doubt, that I should have all that which is requisite.

'And now, dear believing reader, rejoice and praise with me. About an hour, after I had prayed thus, there was given to me the sum of Two Thousand Pounds for the Building Fund. Thus I have received altogether £9,285 3s. 9½d. towards this work. I cannot describe the joy I had in God when I received this donation. It must be known from experience, in order to be felt. 447 days I have had day by day to wait upon God, before the sum reached the above amount. How great is the blessing which the soul obtains by trusting in God, and by waiting patiently. Is it not manifest how precious it is to carry on God's work in this way, even with regard to the obtaining of means?" The total amount which came in for the Building Fund was £15,784 18s. 10d.

Orphan Houses Number 2 and 3

"March 12, 1862. It was in November, 1850, that my mind was beginning actively desire to enlarge the Orphan Work from 300 Orphans to 1000, and subsequently to 1150; and it was in June, 1851 that this my purpose became known after having kept it secret for more than seven months though day by day praying about it. From the end of November, 1850, to this day, March 12, 1862, not one single day has been allowed to pass without this contemplated enlargement being brought before God in prayer often more than once a day. But only now, this day, the new Orphan House No. 3 was so far advanced, that it could be opened.

'Observe then first esteemed reader, how long it may be before a full answer to our prayers is given. Perhaps until thousands and tens of thousands of prayers are granted; even though those prayers may be believing prayers, earnest prayers, and offered up in the name of the Lord Jesus. And though we may only for the sake of the honor of our Lord desire the answer as I did, by the grace of God without the least doubt and wavering, I still looked for more than eleven years for the full answer seeking only the glory of God."

Praying Three Times Daily for Helpers

"As in the case of Number 2, it was so also in the case of the New Orphan House Number 3, I had prayed daily for the needed helpers and assistants for the various departments. Before a stone was laid, I began to pray for this; and as the building progressed I continued day by day to bring this matter before God, feeling assured that as in everything else, so also in this particular work He would again be graciously pleased to appear on our behalf and help us, for the whole work is intended for His honor and glory.

WHEN EXPECTED HELP DID NOT ARRIVE

"At last the time was near when the house could be opened, and the time drew near when the applications that had been made in writing during more than two years previously, should be considered for the filling up of the various posts. It was now found, however, that while there had been about 50 applications made for the various situations some places could not be filled up because either the individuals who had applied for them were married, or were on examination found unsuitable. This was no small trial of faith; for day by day for years I had asked God to help me in this particular need even as He had done in the case of the New Orphan House Number 2.

'I had also expected help, *confidently* expected help: and yet now, when help seemed needed it was wanting. What was to be done now, dear reader? Would it have been right to charge God with unfaithfulness? Would it have been right to distrust Him? Would it have been right to say, it is useless to pray? By no means. This, on the contrary I did; I thanked God for all the help, He had given me in connection with the whole of the enlargement. I thanked Him for enabling me to overcome so many and such great difficulties. I thanked Him for the helpers He had given me for Orphan House Number 2. I thanked Him; also, for the helpers He had given me already for Number 3.

'And instead of distrusting God, I looked upon this

delay of the full answer to prayer, only as a trial of faith, and therefore resolved that instead of praying once a day with my dear wife about this matter, as we had been doing day by day for years, we should now meet daily three times to bring this before God. I also brought the matter before the whole staff of my helpers in the work requesting their prayers. Thus I have now continued for about four months longer in prayer, day by day, three times a day calling upon God because of this need. And the result has been, that one helper after the other has been given, without the help coming too late, or the work getting into confusion; or the reception of the children being hindered. Once again I am fully assured that the few who are yet needed will also be found when they are really required."

DIFFICULTIES REMOVED AFTER PRAYER AND PATIENCE

Mr. Müeller relates the following incidents in connection with the purchase of the land for the Fourth and Fifth Orphan Houses, after receiving five thousand pounds for the Building Fund:

"I had now through all that had come in since May 26th, 1864, including this last mentioned donation more than Twenty-Seven Thousand Pounds in hand. I had patiently waited on God's time. I had determined to do nothing until I had the full half of the sum needed for the two houses. But now having more than Two Thousand Pounds beyond the half I felt quite happy in taking steps for the purchase of the land after again seeking counsel from God.

'For years my eyes had been directed to a beautiful piece of land separated only by the turnpike road from the ground on which the New Orphan

House No. 3 is erected. The land is about 18 acres, with a small house and outhouses built on one end of it. Hundreds of times I had prayed within the last years that God for Jesus' sake would count me worthy to be allowed to erect two more Orphan Houses on this ground; and hundreds of times I had with a prayerful eye looked on this land and covered it with drops of tears by my prayers.

'I could have bought it years ago; but that would have been going before the Lord. I had money enough in hand to have paid for it years ago; but I desired patiently, and submissively to wait on God's own time and for Him to mark it clearly and distinctly that His time was come. I needed to take the step according to His will; for whatever I might apparently accomplish, if the work were mine, and not the Lord's, I could expect no blessing. But now the Lord's mind was clearly and distinctly made manifest. I had enough money in hand to pay for the land and to build one house, and therefore I went forward, after having still asked the Lord for guidance, and being assured that it was His will I should take active steps."

A FURTHER DIFFICULTY

"The first thing I did was to see the agent who acted for the owner of the land, and to ask him whether the land was for sale. He replied that it was, but that it was leased until March 25th, 1867. He said that he would write for the price. Here a great difficulty at once presented itself, the land was leased for two years and four months longer. Now while it appeared desirable that I would be able to take possession of it in about six months so the conveyance could be made out and the plans made ready for the New Orphan House No. 4, with the contractors, we have a further difficulty. But I was not discouraged by this difficulty; for I expected through prayer to make happy and satisfactory arrangements with the tenant, being willing to give him a fair compensation for leaving before his time had expired. But, before I had time to see about this, two other great difficulties presented themselves: the one was, that the owner asked £7,000 for the land, which I judged to be considerably more than its value; and the other, that I heard that the Bristol Waterworks Company intended to make an additional reservoir for their water, on this very land, and to get an Act of Parliament passed to that effect.

'Pause here for a few moments, esteemed reader. You have seen, how the Lord brought me thus far with regard to financial means that I felt now warranted to go forward; and I may further add, that I was brought to this point as the result of thousands of times praying regarding this object. And that there were many hundreds of children waiting for admission; and yet, after the Lord himself so manifestly had appeared on our behalf, by the donation of £5,000, He allows this apparent death blow to come upon the whole project.

'But as I have found it hundreds of times since I have known the Lord, the difficulties that He is pleased to allow to arise are only allowed under such circumstances for the exercise of our faith and patience. More prayer, more patience, and the exercise of faith will remove the difficulties. Now, as I knew the Lord, these difficulties were no insurmountable difficulties to me, for I put my trust in Him, according to that word: *"The Lord also will be a refuge for the oppressed, a refuge in times of trouble. And they that know Thy name will put their trust in Thee: for Thou, Lord, hast not forsaken them that seek Thee"* (Psalm 9:9-10). Therefore, I gave myself earnestly to prayer concerning all these three special difficulties that had arisen regarding the land. I prayed several times daily about the matter, and used the following means:

1. I saw the Acting Committee of the Directors of the Bristol Waterworks Company regarding their intended reservoir on the land that I was about to purchase, and stated to them what I had seen in print concerning their intentions. They courteously stated to me that only a small portion of the land would be required, not enough to interfere with my purpose and that if it could be avoided even this small portion would not be taken.

2. This being settled, I now saw the tenant after many prayers; for I desired as a Christian that if this land were bought it should be done under amicable circumstances with regard to him. At the first interview I stated my intentions to him at the same time expressing my desire that the matter should be settled pleasantly with regard to him. He said that he would consider the matter, and desired a few days for that purpose. After a week I saw him again, and he then kindly stated that as the land was wanted for such an object he would not stand in the way; but that as he had laid out a good deal of money on the house and land, he expected a compensation for leaving it before his time was up. I was of course quite willing to give a fair and reasonable compensation. I considered this a very precious answer to prayer.

3. I now entered upon the third difficulty, the price of the land. I knew well how much the land was worth to the Orphan Institution; but its value to the Institution was not the market value. Therefore, I gave myself day by day to prayer asking the Lord to constrain

the owner to accept a considerably lower sum than he had asked. I also pointed out to him why it was not worth as much as he asked. At last he consented to take £5,500 instead of £7,000, and I accepted the offer for I knew that by the level character of the land we would save a considerable sum for the two houses, and the new sewer that only a few months before had been completed running along under the turnpike road near the field would be a considerably benefit. In addition to these two points I had to take into the account that we can have gas from Bristol like the three houses already in operation.

And lastly, the most important point of all, the nearness of this piece of land to the other three houses, enabled them to be under the same direction and superintendence. In fact, no other piece of land, near or far off, would present so much advantage to us as this spot that the Lord so very kindly had given to us. All being now settled, I proceeded to have the land conveyed to the same trustees who stood trustees for the New Orphan Houses Number 1, Number 2, and Number 3. I have thus minutely dwelt on these various matters for the encouragement of the readers that they may not be discouraged by difficulties however great and many and varied, but give themselves to prayer, trusting in the Lord for help, yes and expecting help, which in His own time and way He will surely grant."

Orphan Houses Number 4 and 5

"March 5, 1874. Both houses Number 4 and 5 have now been on operation for years. Number 4 since November, 1868, and Number 5, since the beginning of the year 1870. More than 1,200 Orphans have been already received into them and month after month more are received, as the

Orphans are sent out from them as apprentices or servants.

'Moreover all the expenses in connection with their being built, fitted up and furnished were met to the full, as the demands arose, and after all had been paid there was left a balance of several thousand pounds that is being used for keeping the houses in repair.

'See how abundantly God answered our prayers, esteemed Reader, and how plain it is, that we were not mistaken after we had patiently and prayerfully sought to ascertain His will. Be encouraged, therefore, to further and further confide in the Living God."

Chapter 3

PRECIOUS ANSWERS TO PRAYER

In remarkable ways God helped
Mr. Müeller as "The Narratives" show:

THE ARTIST'S FIRST SALE IN BRISTOL

APRIL 30 1859. I received the following letter from a considerable distance: 'My dear Christian Brother, I am the husband of Mrs. ---- who sends you by this post the two Sovereign pieces. How can we better dispose of this relic of affectionate remembrance, than by depositing it in the bank of Christ, who always pays the best interest, and never fails. Now, my best and spiritual counselor, I cannot express to you the exceeding great joy I feel in relating what follows. I am an artist, a poor artist, a landscape painter. About two weeks ago I sent a picture to Bristol for exhibition, just as I finished your book that was lent us. I most humbly and earnestly prayed to God to enable me, by the sale of my Bristol picture, to have the blessed privilege of sending you half the proceeds. The price of the picture is £20.

'Now mark this. Immediately when the exhibition opened, God, in His mercy and mindful of my prayer sends me a purchaser. I have exhibited in Bristol before, but never sold a picture. Oh! My dear friend, my very heart leaps for joy. I have never been so near God before. Through your instrumentality I have been enabled to draw nearer to God with more earnestness, more faith, and more holy desires. This is the first sale God has blessed me with for the whole of my last year's labors. What a blessing to have it done so!

Oh, with what joy I read your book! The picture I speak of is now being exhibited in the academy of arts at Clifton, numbered in the Catalog ----, the title is ----. I cannot pay you till the close of the exhibition, as I shall not be paid till then, etc.' I have had thousands of such letters during the last 40 years."

THE NORTH WIND CHANGED INTO A SOUTH WIND

"It was towards the end of November of 1857, when I was most unexpectedly informed that the boiler of our heating apparatus at Orphan House Number 1 leaked very considerably, so that it was impossible to go through the winter with such a leak. Our heating apparatus consists of a large cylinder boiler, inside of which the fire is kept, and with which boiler the water pipes that warm the rooms are connected. Hot air is also connected with this apparatus. The boiler had been considered suited for the work of the winter. To suspect that it was worn out, and not to do anything towards replacing it by a new one and to have said I will trust in God regarding it would be careless presumption, not faith in God. It would be the counterfeit of faith.

'The boiler is entirely surrounded by brickwork; its state, therefore, could not be known without taking down the brickwork. This, if it turned out to be not necessary, would be rather injurious to the boiler. For eight winters we had had no difficulty in this way and we had not anticipated it now. But suddenly, and most unexpectedly, at the commencement of the winter, this difficulty occurred. What then was to be done? For the children, especially the younger infants, I felt deeply concerned, that they might not suffer through want of warmth. But how were we to obtain warmth? The introduction of a new boiler would in all probability take many weeks. The repairing of the existing boiler was a questionable matter due to the greatness of the leak. Nothing could be known until the brick chamber in which it is enclosed was at least in part removed; but that would take days; and what was to be done in the meantime to find warm rooms for 300 children?

'It naturally occurred to me, to introduce temporary gas stoves; but on further weighing the matter; it was found that we would be unable to heat our very large rooms with gas except we had many stoves. Also we did not have a sufficient quantity of gas to spare from our lighting apparatus. Not only that, but for each of these stoves we needed a small chimney, to carry off the impure air. This mode of heating, therefore, though applicable to a hall, a staircase, or a shop, would not suit our purpose.

'I also thought of the temporary introduction of Arnott's stoves; but they would have been unsuitable because they required long chimneys (as they would have been of a temporary kind) to go out of the windows. Not to mention the disfigurement of the rooms, therefore, we gave up on this plan also. But what was to be done? I would gladly have paid £100, if thereby the difficulty could have been overcome, and the children not be exposed to suffer for many days from being in cold rooms. At last I determined on falling entirely into the hands of God, who is very merciful and of tender compassion, and I decided on having the brick-chamber opened, to see the extent of the damage, and whether the boiler might be repaired to carry us through the winter.

'The day was fixed, when the workmen were to come, and all the necessary arrangements were made. The fire, of course, had to be put out while the repairs were going on. But now see. After the day was fixed for the repairs a bleak North wind set in. It began to blow either on Thursday or

Friday before the Wednesday afternoon, when the fire was to be let put out. Now came the first really cold weather, which we had in the beginning of that winter, during the first days of December. What was to be done? The repairs could not be put off. I now asked the Lord for two things. That He would be pleased to change the north wind into a south wind, and that He would give to the workmen 'a mind to work'; for I remembered how much Nehemiah accomplished in 52 days, while building the walls of Jerusalem, because 'the people had a mind to work.'

'Well, the memorable day came. The evening before, the bleak north wind blew still: but, on the Wednesday, the south wind blew: exactly as I had prayed. The weather was so mild that no fire was needed. The brickwork is removed, the leak is found out very soon, the boiler makers begin to repair in good earnest. About half-past eight in the evening, when I was going home, I was informed at the lodge, that the acting principal of the firm, whence the boiler makers came, had arrived to see how the work was going on, and whether he could in any way speed the matter. I went immediately, therefore, into the cellar, to see him with the men to expedite the business. In speaking to the principal of this, he said in their hearing, 'the men will work late this evening, and come very early again tomorrow."

"'We would rather, Sir,' said the leader, 'work all night.' Then I remembered the second part of my prayer that God would give the men 'a mind to work.' Thus it was: by the morning the repair was accomplished, the leak was stopped, though with great difficulty, and within about 30 hours the brickwork was up again, and the fire in the boiler; and all the time the south wind blew so mildly, that there was not the least need of a fire."

"'Here, then, is one of our difficulties that were overcome by prayer and faith."

CONVERSION OF THE ORPHANS

"May 26, 1860. Day after day and year after year, by the help of God, we labor in prayer for the spiritual benefit of the Orphans under our care. These our supplications, which for 24 years have been brought before the Lord concerning them, have been abundantly answered, in former years, in the conversion of hundreds among them. We have also had repeated seasons in which, within a short time or all at once, many of the Orphans were converted. Such a season as that we had about three years ago when within a few days about 60 were brought to believe in the Lord Jesus; and such seasons we also had twice during the first year. The first was in July, 1859, when the Spirit of God wrought so mightily in one school of 120 girls that very many in fact more than half were brought under deep concern about the salvation of their souls. This work was not a mere momentary excitement; but after more than eleven months have elapsed there are 31 with whom we have full confidence as to their conversion, and 32 more with whom we have a measure of confidence. There are, therefore, 63 out of the 120 Orphans in that one School who are considered to have been converted in July, 1859.

'This blessed and mighty work of the Holy Spirit cannot be traced to any particular cause. It was however, a most precious answer to prayer. As such we look upon it, and are encouraged by it to further waiting upon God. The second season of the mighty working of the Holy Spirit among the Orphans during the past year was at the end of January and the beginning of February, 1860. The particulars of it are of the deepest interest; but I must content myself by stating that this great work of the Spirit of God in January and February, 1860, began among the younger class of the children under our care, little girls of about 6, 7, 8 and 9 years old. This working of the Holy Spirit then extended to the older girls; and then to the boys, so that within about 10 days more than 200 of the Orphans were stirred up to be anxious about their souls, and in many instances found peace immediately through faith in our Lord Jesus. They at once requested to be allowed to hold prayer meetings among themselves, and have had these meetings ever since. Many of them also manifested a concern about the salvation of their companions and relations, and spoke or wrote to them about the way to be saved."

APPRENTICING THE ORPHANS

"In the early part of the summer of 1862, it was found that we had several boys ready to be apprenticed; but there were no applications made by masters for apprentices. As all our boys are invariably sent out as indoor apprentices, this was no small difficulty; for we not only look for Christian masters, but consider their business and examine their position to see whether they are suitable. The master must also be willing to receive the apprentice into his own family. Under these circumstances, we again gave ourselves to prayer. We had been doing this for more than twenty years instead of advertising, which, in all probability, would only bring before us masters who desire apprentices for the sake of the premium. We remembered how good the Lord had been to us by having helped us hundreds of times before in this very matter.

'Some weeks passed, but the difficulty remained. We continued, however, in prayer and then one application was made, and then another; and since we first began to pray about this matter last summer we have been able to send out altogether 18 boys as of May 26, 1863. The difficulty was once more entirely overcome by prayer for every one of the boys whom it was desirable to send out has been sent."

SICKNESS AT THE ORPHANAGE

"Sickness at times visited the houses. During the summer and autumn of 1866 we had the measles at all the three Orphan Houses. After they had made their appearance our special prayer was:

1. That there might not be too many children ill at one time in this disease, so that our accommodation in the Infirmary rooms or otherwise might be sufficient. This prayer was answered to the full; for though we had at the New Orphan House No. 1 not less than 83 cases, in Number 2 altogether 111, and in Number 3 altogether 68; God was so graciously pleased to listen to our supplications that when our spare rooms were filled with the invalids He stayed the spreading of the measles until a sufficient number were restored to make room for others who were taken ill.

2. Further we prayed that the children who were taken ill with the measles might be safely brought through and not die. Thus it was. We had the full answer to our prayers; for though 262 children altogether had the measles, not one of them died.

3. Lastly we prayed that no evil physical consequences might follow this disease, as is so often the case; this was also granted. All the 262 children not only recovered, but did well afterwards. I gratefully record this special mercy and blessing of God, and this full and precious answer to prayer to the honor of His name."

HELP FOR NEEDY BRETHREN

"1863. The end of the year was now at hand, and in winding up the accounts it was my earnest desire to once more do all I could in sending help to needy laborers in the gospel. Therefore, I went through the list writing the various names of those to whom I had not already recently sent what amount it appeared desirable to send. I found when these sums were added together the total was £476, but £280 was all I had in hand. Therefore, I wrote a check for £280, though I would have gladly sent £476, yet felt thankful at the same time that I had this amount in hand for these brethren.

Having written the check as the last thing I had to do of the day then came my usual season for prayer for the many things that I daily, by the help of God, bring before Him. I then brought the case of these preachers of the Gospel before the Lord, and prayed that He would be pleased to give me a goodly sum for them though there remained only three days to the close of our year. This being done, I went home about nine o'clock in the evening, and found there had arrived from a great distance £100 for Missions, with £100 left at my disposal, and £5 for myself. Therefore, I took the whole £200 for missions and had £480 in hand to meet the £476 which I desired for this object. Those who know the blessedness of really trusting in God, and getting help from Him in answer to prayer will be able to enter into the spiritual enjoyment I had in the reception of that donation in which both the answer to prayer was granted, and with it the great enjoyment of gladdening the hearts of many devoted servants of Christ."

THE HEART'S DESIRE GIVEN TO HELP MISSION WORK IN CHINA

"September 30, 1869. Received from Yorkshire £50. Received also One Thousand Pounds today for the Lord's work in China. About this donation, it is especially to be noticed that for months it had been my earnest desire to do more than ever for Mission Work in China, and I had already taken steps to carry out this desire when this donation of One Thousand Pounds came to hand. This precious answer to prayer for means should be a particular encouragement to all who are engaged in the Lord's work and who may need means for it. It proves afresh that if our work is His work and we honor Him by waiting upon and looking to Him for means, He will surely in His own time and way supply them."

THE JOY OF ANSWERS TO PRAYER

"The joy that answers to prayer give cannot be described and the impetus that they afford to the spiritual life is exceedingly great. I desire this experience of this happiness for all my Christian readers. If you believe indeed in the Lord Jesus for the salvation of your soul, if you walk uprightly and do not regard iniquity in your heart, and if you continue to wait patiently and believingly upon God; then answers will surely be given to your prayers. You may not be called upon to serve the Lord in the way this writer does, and therefore, may never have answers to prayer respecting such things as are recorded here; but, in your various circumstances, your family, your business, your profession, your church position, and your labor for the Lord, etc., you may have answers as distinct as any here recorded."

THE GREAT NEED OF BEING SAVED BY FAITH IN CHRIST JESUS

"If this is read by any who are not believers in the Lord Jesus, and who are going on in the carelessness or self-righteousness of their unrenewed hearts, then I would affectionately and solemnly beseech you, first of all to be reconciled to God by faith in the Lord Jesus. Why? Because you are sinners and you deserve punishment. If you do not see this, ask God to show it unto you. Let this now be your first and most important prayer. Ask God also to enlighten you not merely concerning your state by nature, but especially to reveal the Lord Jesus to your heart.

'God sent Him that He might bear the punishment due to us guilty sinners. God accepts the obedience and sufferings of the Lord Jesus, in the room of those who depend upon Him for the salvation of their souls; and the moment a sinner believes in the Lord Jesus, he obtains the forgiveness of all his sins. When he is reconciled to God by faith in the Lord Jesus and has received the forgiveness of his sins, he has the boldness to enter into the presence of God and to make known his requests unto Him. The more he is enabled to realize that his sins are forgiven, and that God, for Christ's sake, is well pleased with those who believe on Him the more ready he will be to come with all his wants, both temporal and spiritual to his Heavenly Father that He may supply them.

'But as long as the consciousness of unpardoned guilt remains he shall we be kept at a distance from God, especially as it regards prayer. Therefore, dear reader, if you are an unforgiven sinner, let your first, and most important life-changing prayer is that God would reveal His beloved Son, the Lord Jesus Christ, to your heart."

A DOUBLE ANSWER

"July 25, 1865. I received £100 from the neighborhood of London with the following letter:

'My dear Sir, I believe that it is through the Lord's acting upon me, that I enclose you a check on the Bank of England, Western Branch, for £100. I hope that your affairs are going on well.

Yours in the Lord————.'

"This Christian gentleman, whom I have never seen

and who is engaged in a very large business in London, had sent me a similar sum several times before, A day or two before I received this last kind donation, I had asked the Lord if He would influence the heart of this donor to help me again, which I had never done before regarding him; and thus I had the double answer to prayer in that not only money came in, but money from him. 'The reader will now see the meaning in the donor's letter, when he wrote 'I believe that it is through the Lord's acting upon me that I enclose you a check. Truly it was the Lord who acted upon this gentleman to send me this sum.

'Perhaps the reader may think that in acknowledging the receipt of the donation that I may have written the donor what I have here stated. I did not. My reason for not doing so was, lest he should have thought I was in special need, and might have been influenced to send more. In truly knowing the Lord and in really relying upon Him and upon Him alone there is no need of giving hints directly or indirectly whereby individuals may be induced further to help. If I had wanted to I could have hinted to him that I needed a considerable sum day by day for the current expenses of the various objects of the Institution, and I yet needed about Twenty Thousand Pounds to enable me to meet all the expenses connected with the contemplated enlargement of the Orphan work. But my practice is never, never to allude to any of these things in my correspondence with donors. When the Report is published, everyone can see who has a need and desire to see how matters stand. Therefore, I leave things in the hands of God to speak for us to the hearts of His stewards. And this He does. Truly, we do not wait upon God in vain!"

CHRISTIANS IN BUSINESS

"January, 1869. I received £50 from Scotland for Missions, £25 for the circulation of the Holy Scriptures and £25 for the circulation of Tracts. I also received from a considerable distance £10 for these objects, with £10 for the Orphans. About this latter donation I make a few remarks. At the early part of the year 1868, a Christian business man wrote to me for advice in his peculiarly difficult business affairs. His letter showed that he had a desire to walk in the ways of the Lord and to carry on his business to the glory of God; but his circumstances were of the most trying character. I therefore wrote to him to come to Bristol, that I might be able to advise him. Accordingly he undertook the long journey and I had an interview with him through which I learned his most trying position in business. Having fully conversed with him, I gave him the following counsel:

1. That day by day for this express purpose, he retire with his Christian wife that they might unitedly spread their business difficulties before God in prayer. And of possible do this twice a day.

2. That he should look for answers to his prayers, and expect that God would help him.

3. That he should avoid all business trickeries such as exposing for sale two or three articles marked below cost price for the sake of attracting customers. Because it is unbecoming of a disciple of the Lord Jesus to use such artificial means and that if he did so he could not reckon on the blessing of God.

4. I advised him further to set apart out of his profits week by week a certain proportion for the work of God, whether his income was much or little and use this income faithfully for the Lord.

5. Lastly, I asked him to let me know month after month how the Lord dealt with him.

'The reader will be interested to learn that from that time the Lord was pleased to prosper the business of this dear Christian brother, so that his returns from the 1st of March, 1868, up to March 1, 1869, were £9,138 13s. 5d. while during the same period the previous year they had been only £6,609 18s. 3d. Therefore, the Lord brought in £2,528 15s. 2d. more than the year before. When he sent me the donation above referred to, he also wrote that he had been enabled to put aside during the previous year £123 13s. 3d. for the work of God or the need of the poor. I have dwelt fully on this because Christians in business may be benefited by it."

REVIVAL IN THE ORPHAN HOUSES

"In giving the statistics of the previous year 1871-72, I referred already to the great spiritual blessing, which it pleased the Lord to grant to the Orphan Work at the end of that year and the beginning of this year; but, as this is such deeply important subject I wish to enter somewhat further and more fully into it here.

' It was stated before that the spiritual condition of the Orphans generally gave us great sorrow of heart because there were so few comparatively among them who were in earnest about their souls and resting on the atoning death of the Lord Jesus for salvation. Thus, our sorrow led us to lay it on the whole staff of assistants, matrons and teachers, to seek earnestly the Lord's blessing on the souls of the children. This was done in our united prayer meetings and I have reason to believe, in secret also; and in answer to these our secret and united prayers, in the year 1872, there were more believers by far among the Orphans than ever. On January 8, 1872, the Lord began to work among them, and this work was going on more or less afterwards.

'In the New Orphan House Number 3, it showed itself least until the Lord lay His hand heavily on that house by smallpox; and from that time the working of the Holy Spirit was felt in that house particularly in one department. At the end of July, 1872, I received the statements of all the matrons and teachers in the five houses that after careful observation and conversation they had good reason to believe that 729 of the Orphans then under our care were believers in the Lord Jesus. This number of believing Orphans is by far greater than ever we had, for which we adore and praise the Lord! See how the Lord overruled the great trial, occasioned by the smallpox, and turned it into a great blessing! See also how, after knowing how few of orphans were saved, which led us to earnest prayer, the working of the Holy Spirit was more manifest than ever!"

MR. MÜELLER'S MISSION TOURS

In the year 1875, when he was seventy years of age, Mr. Müeller was led to start on his Missionary Tours, and during the next twenty years preached to more than three million people, in forty-two countries of the world.

On August 8th, 1882, Mr. Müeller says, "we began our ninth Missionary Tour. The first place at which I preached was Weymouth, where I spoke in public four times. From Weymouth we went by way of Calais and Brussels to Düsseldorf on the Rhine where I preached many times six years before. During this visit, I spoke there in public eight times. Regarding my stay at Düsseldorf, for the encouragement of the reader, I relate the following circumstance. During our first visit to that city, in the year 1876, a godly City Missionary came to me one day, greatly tried because he had six sons for whose conversion he had been praying many years, and yet they remained unconcerned about their soul, and he desired me to tell him what to do. My reply was, 'Continue to pray for your sons, and expect an answer to your prayer, and you will have to praise God.'

'Now, when after six years I was again in the same city, this dear man came to me and said he was surprised he himself had not seen before what he ought to do, and that he had resolved to take my advice and more earnestly than ever give himself to prayer. Two months after he saw me, five of his six sons were converted within eight days and have now walked in the ways of the Lord for six years, and he had hope that the sixth son also was beginning to be concerned about his state before God. May the Christian reader be encouraged by this, for if his prayers are not answered at once, instead of ceasing to pray, wait upon God all the more earnestly and perseveringly and expect answers to his petitions."

THE DIVINE PLAN FOR SENDING OUT FOREIGN MISSIONARIES

The Bristol Church with which Mr. Müeller was connected has been privileged to set an example to the Church of God on the way that greatly needed Foreign Missionaries can be sent forth in answer to prayer. Mr. Müeller writes in his Narrative:

"I also mention here, that during the eight years prior to my going to Germany to labor, it had been laid on my heart and on the hearts of some other brethren among us to ask the Lord to honor us as a body of believers by calling forth brethren from our midst to carrying the truth into foreign lands. But this prayer seemed to remain unanswered. 'Now, however, the time was come when the Lord was about to answer it. I, on whose heart this matter had been laid was to be the first to carry forth the truth from among us.

'About that very time the Lord called our dear brother and sister Barrington from among us, to go to Demerara to labor there in connection with our esteemed brother Strong. Our dear brother and sister Espenett were to go to Switzerland. Both these dear brethren and sisters left very shortly after I had gone to Germany. But this was not all. Our much valued brother Mordal, who had commended himself to the saints by his unwearied faithful service among us for twelve years, had his mind likewise set on doing service in Demerara since August 31, 1843, the day on which brothers Strong and Barrington sailed from Bristol for Demerara. Therefore, he left for Demerara eleven months later. He and I had it particularly laid upon our hearts during the previous eight years to ask the Lord again and again to call laborers from among us for Foreign Service. Of all persons he, the father of a large family and about 50 years of age seemed like the least likely to be called to that work; but God did call him. He labored a little while in Demerara, and then on January 9, 1845, the Lord took him to his rest in Him.

'When we ask God to raise up laborers for His harvest, or send means for the carrying on of His work, the honest questions to be put to our hearts should be these: Am I willing to go, if He should call me? Am I willing to give according to my ability? For we may be the very persons whom the Lord will call for the work, or whose means He may wish to employ.

'In the Report of the Scriptural Knowledge Institution for 1896, Mr. Müeller shows how greatly this body of believers has been honored by God:

"From our own midst as a church, sixty brethren

and sisters have gone forth to foreign fields of labor, some of whom have finished their labor on earth; but there are still about forty yet engaged in this precious service. Why should not the great and crying need for workers in Asia, Africa, and other parts of the world be thus met by thousands of churches in Europe and America following this divine plan of praying and asking the Lord of the harvest to send forth laborers from among them? Surely they may expect God to answer their prayers as He did the prayers of this Bristol church. Look what has been done in China by the faithful use of GOD'S method!"

QUOTE FROM HUDSON TAYLOR IN CHINA INLAND MISSION

We quote Mr. Hudson Taylor's words as given in *China's Millions* for July, 1897:

"For the obtaining of fellow workers we took the Master's direction in Matthew 9:38, Pray *ye therefore the Lord of the harvest that he will send forth labourers into his harvest*. As for the first five before the Mission was formed, so also, for the twenty-four for whom we first asked for the C.I.M. for further reinforcements when they were needed. For the seventy in three years; for the hundred in one year, and for further additions from time to time we have always relied on this plan. Is it possible that in any other way such a band of workers from nearly every denomination, and from many lands, could have been gathered and kept together for thirty years with no other bond save that which the call of God and the love of God has proved--a band now numbering over seven hundred men and women, aided by more than five hundred native workers."

The Beginning of the 1859 Revival

"In November, 1856, a young Irishman, Mr. James McQuilkin, was brought to the knowledge of the Lord. Soon after his conversion he saw my Narrative in the first two volumes of this book. He had a great desire to read it, and procured it accordingly, about January, 1857. God blessed it greatly to his soul, especially in showing to him, what could be obtained by prayer. He said to himself something like this: 'See what Mr. Müeller obtains simply by prayer. Thus I may obtain blessing by prayer.' He now set himself to pray, that the Lord would give him a spiritual companion, one who knew the Lord. Soon after he became acquainted with a young man who was a believer. These two began a prayer meeting in one of the Sunday Schools in the parish of Connor.

'Having had his prayer answered in obtaining a spiritual companion, Mr. James McQuilkin asked the Lord to lead him to become acquainted with some more of His hidden ones. Soon after the Lord gave him two more young men, who were believers previously, as far as he could judge. In autumn of 1857, Mr. James McQuilkin stated to these three young men given him in answer to believing prayer what blessing he had derived from my Narrative. How it had led him to see the power of believing prayer; and he proposed that they should meet for prayer to seek the Lord's blessing upon their various labors in the Sunday Schools, prayer meetings, and preaching of the Gospel.

'Accordingly in autumn, 1857, these four young men met together for prayer every Friday evening in a small schoolhouse near the village of Kells, in the parish of Connor. By this time the great and mighty working of the Spirit, in 1857, in the United States, had become known, and Mr. James McQuilkin said to himself, 'Why may not we have such a blessed work here, seeing that God did such great things for Mr. Müeller simply in answer to prayer?

'On January 1, 1858, the Lord gave them the first remarkable answer to prayer in the conversion of a farm servant. He was taken into the number, and thus there were five who gave themselves to prayer. Shortly after, another young man about 20 years old was converted; there were now six. This greatly encouraged the other three who first had met with Mr. James McQuilkin. Others were now converted who were also taken into the number; but only believers were admitted to these fellowship meetings in which they read, prayed, and offered to each other a few thoughts from the Scriptures. These meetings and others for the preaching of the Gospel were held in the parish of Connor, Antrim, Ireland. Up to this time all was going on most quietly, though many souls were converted. There were no physical prostrations, as afterwards occurred."

"Around Christmas, 1858, a young man, from Ahoghill, who had come to live at Connor, and who had been converted through this little company of believers, went to see his friends at Ahoghill and spoke to them about their own souls and the work of God at Connor. His friends desired to see some of these converts. Accordingly Mr. James McQuilkin, with two of the first who met for prayer, went on February 2, 1859, and held a meeting at Ahoghill in one of the Presbyterian Churches. Some believed, some mocked, and others thought there was a great deal of presumption in these young converts; yet many wished to have another meeting. This was held by the same three young men on February 16th, 1859; and now the Spirit of God began to work, and to work mightily. Souls were converted, and from that time conversions multiplied rapidly. Some of these converts went to other places, and carried the spiritual fire, so to speak, with them. The blessed work of the spirit of

God spread in many places.

'On April 5, 1859, Mr. James McQuilkin went to Ballymena and held a meeting there in one of the Presbyterian Churches. On April 11, he held another meeting in another of the Presbyterian churches where several were convinced of sin and the work of the Spirit of God went forward in Ballymena. On May 28, 1859, he went to Belfast and during the first week there were meetings held in five different Presbyterian Churches, and from that time the blessed work commenced at Belfast. In all these visits he was accompanied and helped by Mr. Jeremiah Meneely, one of the three young men who first met with him after the reading of my Narrative. From this time the work of the Holy Ghost spread further and further as the young converts were used by the Lord to carry the truth from one place to another.

'Such was the beginning of that mighty work of the Holy Spirit that has led to the conversion of hundreds of thousands. Some of my readers will remember how in 1859 this fire was kindled in England, Wales and Scotland, and how it spread through Ireland, England, Wales and Scotland until the Continent of Europe was more or less partaking of this mighty working of the Holy Spirit. It led thousands to give themselves to the work of Evangelists; and up to the year 1874, not only the effects of this work first begun in Ireland were felt, but that still this blessed work is going on in Europe. It is almost needless to add, that in no degree the honor is due to the instruments, but to the Holy Spirit alone; yet these facts are stated in order that it may be seen what delight God has in answering abundantly the believing prayer of His children."

MR. MÜELLER'S MARRIAGE

In Volume 3 of The Narrative, Mr. Müeller shows the will of God in his meeting with and subsequent marriage to his first wife, Miss Mary Groves.

"In giving her to me, I own the hand of God; nay, His hand was most marked; and my soul says, 'Thou art good, and doest good.'

'I refer to a few particulars for the instruction of others. At the end of the year 1829, I left London to labor in Devonshire in the Gospel, and a brother in the Lord gave me a card containing the address of a well-known Christian lady, Miss Paget in order that I should call on her as she was an excellent Christian. She then resided in Exeter and I took this address and put it into my pocket, but thought little of calling on her. Three weeks I carried this card in my pocket, without making an effort to see this lady; but at last I was led to do so. This was God's way of giving me my excellent wife. Miss Paget asked me to preach the last Tuesday in the month of January, 1830, at the room which she had fitted up at Poltimore, a village near Exeter, and where Mr. A. N. Groves, afterwards my brother-in-law, had preached once a month before he went out as a Missionary to Bagdad. I readily accepted the invitation as I longed to set forth everywhere the precious truth of the Lord's return and other deeply important truths that not long before my own soul had been filled with.

'On leaving Miss Paget, she gave me the address of a Christian brother, Mr. Hake, who had an Infant Boarding School for young ladies and gentlemen at Northernhay House, the former residence of Mr. A.N. Groves, so that that I might stay there on my arrival in Exeter from Teignmouth. I went to this place at the appointed time and Miss Groves, afterwards my beloved wife was there; for Mrs. Hake had been an invalid for a long time, and Miss Groves helped Mr. Hake by superintending his household matters.

'My first visit led to my going again to preach at Poltimore after a month had lapsed and I stayed again at

Mr. Hake's house; and this second visit led to my preaching once a week in a chapel at Exeter. Thus I went, week after week, from Teignmouth to Exeter, each time staying in the house of Mr. Hake. All this time my purpose had been, not to marry at all, but to remain free for travelling about in the service of the Gospel; but after some months I saw, for many reasons, that it was better for me, as a young Pastor, under 25 years of age to be married. The question now was to whom shall I be united? Miss Groves was before my mind; but the prayerful conflict was long, before I came to a decision; for I could not bear the thought that I would take away from Mr. Hake this valued helper, as Mrs. Hake continued still unable to take the responsibility of so large a household. But I prayed again and again. At last I made a decision for I had reason to believe that I had begotten an affection in the heart of Miss Groves, and that therefore I ought to make a proposal of marriage to her. I asked God to give Mr. Hake a suitable helper to succeed Miss Groves even though it might seem an unkindly act to my dear friend and brother Mr. Hake.

'On August 15, 1830, I therefore wrote to her and proposed to her to become my wife, and on August 19, when I went over as usual to Exeter for preaching, she accepted me. The first thing we did, after I was accepted, was, to fall on our knees, and ask the blessing of the Lord on our intended union. In about two or three weeks the Lord, in answer to prayer, found an individual who seemed suitable to act as housekeeper while Mrs. Hake continued ill; and on October 7, 1830, we were united in marriage. Our marriage was of the most simple character. We walked to church, had no wedding breakfast, but in the afternoon had a meeting of Christian friends in Mr. Hake's house and commemorated the Lord's death; and then I drove off in the stagecoach with my beloved bride to Teignmouth, and the next day we went to work for the Lord. Simple as our beginning was, and unlike the habits of the world, for the sake of Christ. So our Godly aim has been to continue ever since.

'Now see the hand of God in giving me my dearest wife:

First, that address of Miss Paget's was given to me under the ordering of God.

Second, I must at last be made to call on her, though I had long delayed it.

Third, she might have provided a resting place with some other Christian friend, where I would not have seen Miss Groves.

Fourth, my mind might have decided not to make a proposal to her; but God settled the matter by speaking to me through my conscience—*you know that you have begotten affection in the heart of this Christian sister by the way you have acted towards her, and therefore, painful though it may be to appear to act unkindly towards your friend and brother, you ought to make her a proposal.* I obeyed. I wrote the letter in which I made the proposal, and nothing but one even stream of blessing has been the result.

'Let me add here a word of Christian counsel. To enter upon the marriage union is one of the most deeply important events of life. It cannot be too prayerfully treated. Our happiness, our usefulness, our living for God or for ourselves afterwards, are often most intimately connected with our choice. Therefore, this choice should be made in the most prayerful manner. Neither beauty, nor age, nor money, nor mental powers, should be that which prompt the decision; but first, much waiting upon God for guidance should be used. Second, a hearty purpose to be willing to be guided by Him should be aimed after. Third, godliness without a shadow of doubt should be the first and absolutely needful qualification to a Christian with regard to a companion for life. In addition to this, however, it ought to be at the same time calmly and patiently weighed if in all respects there is a suitableness. For instance, for an educated man to choose an entirely uneducated woman is unwise; for however much on his part love might be willing to cover the defect; it will work very unhappily with regard to the children."

DANGEROUS ILLNESS OF MR. MÜELLER'S DAUGHTER

"In July, 1853, it pleased the Lord to try my faith in a way in that it had not been before. My beloved daughter and only child, and a believer since the commencement of the year 1846, was taken ill on June 20th.

'This illness, at first a low fever, turned to typhus. On July 3rd there seemed no hope of her recovery. Now was the trial of faith. But faith triumphed. My beloved wife and I were enabled to give her up into the hands of the Lord. He sustained us both exceedingly. But I will only speak about myself. Though my only and beloved child was brought near the grave yet was my soul in perfect peace, satisfied with the will of my Heavenly Father, being assured that He would only do that for her and her parents, which in the end would be the best. She continued very ill till about July 20th, when restoration began.

'On August 18, though exceedingly weak, she was so far restored that she could be removed to Clevedon for a change of air. It was then 59 days since she was first taken ill. Parents know what an only child, a beloved child is, and what to believing parents an only child, a believing child must be. Well, the Father in Heaven said, as it were, by this His dispensation, 'Art thou willing to give up this child to me?' My heart responded, 'As it seems good to thee, my Heavenly Father, thy will be done.' But as our hearts were made willing to give back our beloved child to Him who had given her to us, so He was ready to leave her to us, and she lived. *'Delight thyself also in the Lord; and He shall give thee the desires of thine heart.'* Psalm 37:4. The desires of my heart were, to retain the beloved daughter if it were the will of God; the means to retain her were to be satisfied with the will of the Lord.

'Of all the trials of faith that as yet I have had to pass through, this was the greatest; and by God's abundant mercy, I own it to His praise, I was enabled to delight myself in the will of God; for I felt perfectly sure, if the Lord took this beloved daughter, it would be best for her parents, best for herself, and more for the glory of God than if she lived. This better part I was satisfied with; and thus my heart had peace, perfect peace, and I had not a moment's anxiety. Thus would it be under all circumstances, however painful, was the believer exercising faith.

THE DAILY BREAD

"August 3, 1844. Saturday. With 12s. We began the day. My soul said: 'I will now look out for the way in which the Lord will deliver us this day again; for He will surely deliver. Many Saturdays, when we were in need, He helped us, and so He will do this day also.' Between nine and ten o'clock this morning I gave myself to prayer for means, with three of my fellow laborers, in my house. *While we were in prayer*, there was a knock at my room door, and I was informed that a gentleman had come to see me. When we had finished prayer, it was found to be a brother from Tetbury, who had brought from Barnstaple £1 2s. 6d. for the Orphans. Thus we have £1 14s. 6d, with which I must return the letter bag to the Orphan Houses, looking to the Lord for more.

"August 6. Without one single penny in my hands the day began. The post brought nothing, nor had I yet received anything, when ten minutes after ten this morning the letter bag was brought from the Orphan Houses, for the supplies of today. Now see the Lord's deliverance! In the bag I found a note from one of the laborers in the Orphan Houses, enclosing two sovereigns that she sent for the Orphans, stating that it was part of a present which she had just received unexpectedly for herself. Thus we are supplied for today."

'"September 4. Only one farthing was in my hands this morning. Pause a moment, dear reader! Only one farthing in hand when the day commenced, think of this, and think of nearly 140 persons to be provided for. You, who are poor brethren having six or eight children and small wages, think of this. And you, my brethren who do not belong to the working classes, but have very limited means, think of this! May you not do what we do while going through your trials? Does the Lord love you less than He loves us? Does He not love all His children with no less love than that, with which He loves His only begotten Son, according to John 17: 20-23? Or are we better than you? No, for are we not in ourselves poor miserable sinners as you are; and have any of the children of God any claim upon God on account of their own worthiness? Is not that, which alone makes us worthy to receive anything from our Heavenly Father, the righteousness of the Lord Jesus that is imputed to those who believe in Him? Therefore, dear reader, as we pray tour Father in Heaven for help in our every need whatever it may be in connection with this work, and as He does help us, so He is also willing to help all His children who put their trust in Him."

'Well, let us hear then, how God helped when there was only one farthing left in my hands, on the morning of September 4, 1844.

'A little after nine o'clock I received a sovereign from

a sister in the Lord, who does not wish the name of the place where she resides mentioned. Between ten and eleven o'clock the bag was sent from the Orphan Houses in which in a note it was stated that £1 2s. was required for today. *Scarcely had I read this,* when a fly [a horse-drawn carriage] stopped before my house, and a gentleman, Mr. ----, from the neighborhood of Manchester, was announced. I found that he was a believer, who had come on business to Bristol. He had heard about the Orphan Houses, and expressed his surprise that without any regular system of collections and without personal application to anyone but simply by faith and prayer obtained £2,000 and more yearly for the work of the Lord in my hands. This brother, whom I had never seen before; and whose name I did not even know before he came, gave me £2, as an exemplification of what I had stated to him."

FOR YE HAVE THE POOR ALWAYS WITH YOU —MARK 14:7

"February 12, 1845. After I had sent off this morning the money which was required for the housekeeping of today, I had again only 16s. 2½d. left, being only about one-fourth as much as is generally needed for one day merely for housekeeping, so that there was now again a fresh call for trusting in the Lord. In the morning, I met again as usual with my dear wife and her sister for prayer to ask the Lord for many blessings in connection with this work, and for means also.

'About one hour after prayer, I received a letter from Devonshire containing an order for £22 of which £10 was for the Orphans, £2 for a poor brother in Bristol, and £10 for me. Besides having thus a fresh proof of the willingness of our Heavenly Father to answer our requests on behalf of the Orphans there is also this to be noticed. For many of the past months the necessities of the poor saints among us have been particularly laid upon my heart. The Word of our Lord: *'Ye have the poor with you always,'* and *'whensoever ye will ye may do them good,'* has again and again stirred me up to prayer on their behalf, and thus it was again in particular this morning. It was the coldest morning we have had the whole winter. In my morning walk for prayer and meditation I thought how well I was supplied with coals, nourishing food, and warm clothing, and how many of the dear children of God might be in need. I then lifted up my heart to God to give me more means for myself, that I might be able to show more abundant sympathy with the poor believers in their need by definite actions on my part, and it was just three hours later when I received this £10 for myself.'"

THE LORD DIRECTING THE STEPS

"February 1, 1847. Before breakfast I took a direction in my usual morning's walk, in which I had not been for many weeks, as I felt drawn in that direction as if God had an intention in leading me in that way. While returning home I met a Christian gentleman whom I used to meet almost every morning, but whom I had not met for many weeks, because I had not been walking in that direction. He stopped me and gave me £2 for the Orphans. Then I knew why I had been led in that direction, for there is not yet enough in hand to supply the matrons tomorrow evening with the necessary means for housekeeping during another week.

'February 4. Yesterday nothing had come in. This morning just before I was going to give myself to prayer about the Orphans, a sister in the Lord sent a sovereign, which she had received, as she writes, 'From a friend who had met the Orphan Boys and was particularly pleased with their neat and orderly appearance.' After having received this £1, I prayed for means for present use, though not confining my prayers to that. About a quarter of an hour after I had risen from my knees, I received a Setter [Money of an unknown origin called *English Saxons* and previously called *Old Saxons*.], with an order for £5. The donor writes that it is 'the proceeds of a strip of land sold to the railway company.' What various means does the Lord employ to send us help, in answer to our prayers!"

CONTINUED TRIALS OF FAITH AND PATIENCE

With the enlargement of the work, by which some 330 persons needed to be provided for, the trials of faith continued. Mr. Müeller writes:

"If we formerly had no certain income, so now have we none. We have to look to God for everything in connection with the work, of which often, however, the pecuniary necessities are the smallest matter; but to Him we are enabled to look, and therefore, we are not disappointed.

'October 7, 1852. This evening there was only £8 left in hand for the current expenses for the Orphans. Hitherto we had generally abounded. But though much had come in, since the commencement of this new period, yet our expenses had been greater than our income as every donation I had put to the Building Fund. Therefore, the balance in hand on May 26, 1852, notwithstanding the large income since then, was reduced to about £8. I therefore gave myself particularly to prayer for means that this small sum might be increased.

'October 9. This morning, the Book of Luke, chapter 7 was in the course of my reading before breakfast. While reading the account about the Centurion and the raising from death of the widow's son at Nain, I lifted up my heart to the Lord Jesus and prayed thus: 'Lord Jesus, Thou hast the same power now. Thou canst provide me with means for Thy work in my hands. Be pleased to do so.' About half an hour afterwards I received £230 15s.

'The joy that such answers to prayer afford cannot be described. I was determined to wait upon God only, and not to work an unscriptural deliverance for myself. I have thousands of pounds for the Building Fund; but I would not take of this sum because it was once set apart for that object. There is also a legacy of £100 for the Orphans two months overdue, in the prospect of the payment of which the heart might be naturally inclined to use some money of the Building Fund, to be replaced by the legacy money, when it comes in; but I would not step out of God's way of obtaining help. At the very time when this donation arrived, I happened to have in hand £100 received for the Building Fund and packed up in order to take it to the Bank, as I was determined not to touch it, but to wait upon God. My soul does magnify the Lord for His goodness.

'June 13, 1853. We were now very poor. Not indeed in debt, nor was all the money gone; for there was still about £12 in hand. But flour was needed to be bought, of which we buy generally 10 sacks at a time, 300 stones of oatmeal, 4 cwt. of soap, and there were many little repairs going on in the house with a number of workmen in addition to the regular current expenses of about £70 per week. Over and above all this, on Saturday, the day before yesterday, I found that the heating apparatus needed to be repaired, which would cost in all probability £25. It was therefore desirable, humanly speaking, to have £100 for these heavy extra expenses, in addition to the means for the current expenses.

'But I had no human prospect whatever of getting even 100 pence, much less £100. In addition to this, today was Monday, when generally the income is little. But, in walking to the Orphan House this morning, and praying as I went, I particularly told the Lord in prayer that on this day even though it was Monday, He could send me much. And thus it was. I received this morning £301 for the Lord›s service, wherever it might be most needed. The joy that I had cannot be described. I walked up and down in my room for a long time, tears of joy and gratitude to the Lord raining plentifully over my cheeks, praising and magnifying the Lord for His goodness, and surrendering myself afresh, with all my heart, to Him for His blessed service. I scarcely ever felt more the kindness of the Lord in helping me."

"November 9. Our need of means is now great, very great. The Lord tries our faith and patience. This afternoon, a brother and sister in the Lord from Gloucestershire asked to see me at the New Orphan House, before their tour through the house. After a few minutes I received a sovereign from the sister, which she had been requested to bring to me for the Building Fund; and from herself she gave me £1 for my own personal expenses, and £1 for the Building Fund, and her husband gave me £5 for the Orphans, and £5 for Foreign Missions. Thus the Lord has refreshed my spirit greatly; but I look for more, and need much more."

"November 12. This evening, while praying for means, a little parcel came containing ten sovereigns from a Christian lady living not far from the New Orphan House. This was a very great refreshment to my spirit."

"October 17, 1854. This morning at family prayer, while reading Exodus 5, we learned that just before the deliverance of the Israelites out of Egypt, their trials were greater than ever. They had not only to make the same number of bricks as before, but also to gather stubble, as no straw was given them any longer. This led me, in expounding the portion, to observe that even now the children of God are often in greater trial than ever, just before help and deliverance comes. Immediately after family prayer it was found, that by the morning's post not one penny had come in for the work of the Lord in which I am engaged. We needed much, and though but very little had come in during the three previous days I now to remembered Exodus 5, and put into practice the truths contained therein. In the course of the day nothing was received. In the evening I had, as usual, a season for prayer with my dear wife regarding the various objects of the Scriptural Knowledge Institution, and then we left the New Orphan House for our home.

'When we arrived at our home around nine o'clock, we found that £5 and also 5s. had been sent from Norwich in two Post Office Orders for the Building Fund, and that £8 3s. 11d. had been sent in for Bibles, Tracts, and Reports, which had been sold. This called for thanksgiving. But a little later, between nine and ten o'clock, a Christian gentleman called and gave me £1 for the Orphans and £200 for foreign missions. He had received these sums from an aged Christian woman, whose savings as a servant during her *whole life*, made up the £200. She also recently had left to her a little annual income of about £30 therefore, she felt constrained by the love of Christ to send the savings of her whole life for foreign missions.

'Our special prayer had been again and again, that the Lord would be pleased to send in means for missionary brethren, as I had reason to believe they were in much need of help. At eight o'clock this evening I had particularly besought the Lord to send help for this object. By the last mail I had sent off £40 to British Guiana, to help seven brethren there in some measure. This amount took the last pound in hand for this object. How gladly would I have sent assistance to other brethren also, but I had no more. Now I am in some degree supplied for this object."

"July 12, 1854. Our means were now again reduced to about £30, as only about £150 had come in since June 15. In addition to this, we had very heavy expenses before us. This morning, in reading through the Book of Proverbs, when I came to chapter 22:19, '*That thy trust may be in the Lord....*,' I said in prayer to Him: 'Lord, I do trust in thee; but wilt thou now be pleased to help me; for I am in need of means for the current expenses of all the various objects of the Institution.' By the first delivery of letters I received an order on a London bank for £100, to be used for all the various objects 'as the present need might require.'"

ARE YOU PREPARED FOR ETERNITY?

"In looking over my account books, I meet again and again with the name of one and another who has finished his course. Soon, dear reader, your turn and mine may come. Are you prepared for eternity? Affectionately I press this question upon you. Do not put it away. Nothing is of greater importance than this point; yes, all other things, however important in their place, are of exceedingly small importance in comparison with this matter.

'Do you ask how you may be prepared for eternity, how to be saved, how to obtain the forgiveness of your sins? The answer is, believe in the Lord Jesus, trust in Him, and depend upon Him alone as it regards the salvation of your soul. He was punished by God, in order that we guilty sinners, if we believe in Him, might not be punished. He fulfilled the law of God, and was obedient even unto death, so that we disobedient, guilty sinners, if we believe in Him, might on His account be reckoned righteous by God. Ponder these things, dear reader, if you have never done so before. Through faith in the Lord Jesus alone can we obtain forgiveness of our sins and be at peace with God; but, believing in Jesus, we become through this very faith the children of God. Thus we have God as our Father, and may come to Him for all the temporal and spiritual blessings that we need. Therefore, every one of my readers may obtain answers to prayers, not only to the same extent that we obtain them, but far more abundantly.

'It may be that few, comparatively, of the children of God are called to serve the Lord in the way of establishing Orphan Houses, etc. But all of them are called upon to trust in God, and to rely upon Him in their various positions and circumstances. They are also called to apply the Word of God, faith, and prayer to their family circumstances, their earthly occupation, their afflictions and necessities of every kind, both temporally and spiritually; just as we, by God's help, in some little measure seek to apply the Word of God, faith and prayer to the various objects of the Scriptural Knowledge Institution for Home and Abroad. I encourage you to try it if you have never done so before, and you will see how happy a life it is.

'Truly I prefer by far this life of almost constant trial, as long as I am able to roll all my cares upon my Heavenly Father, and thus become increasingly acquainted with Him, rather than to a life of outward peace and quietness without these constant proofs of His faithfulness, His wisdom, His love, His power, and His overruling providence."

WAITING ONLY UPON GOD

"September 6, 1854. I received from Clerkenwell £50 one–half to be used for missions, and the other half as I thought best. I took the one-half for the support of the Orphans, and find the following remark in my journal respecting this donation: 'What a precious answer to prayer!' Since August 26, we have been day by day coming to the Lord for our daily supplies. Precious, also, on account of Missionary brethren, whom I seek to help, for whom there was nothing in hand when this donation was received.

Mr. Müeller adds a few remarks to this part of the Narrative:

1. 'Should anyone suppose, on account of its having been stated in the previous pages that we were repeatedly brought low as to means, that the Orphans have not had all that was needful for them; we reply that never, since the work has been in existence, has there a mealtime come, but the Orphans have had good nourishing food in sufficient quantity: and never have they needed clothes, but I have had the means to provide them with all they required.

2. Never since the Orphan work has been in existence have I asked one single human being for any help for this work; and yet, unasked for, simply in answer to prayer, from so many parts of the world, as has been stated, the donations have come in, and that very frequently at a time of the greatest need."

Mr. Müeller writes under the date, 1859:

"Every Wednesday evening I meet with my helpers for united prayer; and day by day I have stated seasons, when I seek to bring the work with its great variety of spiritual and temporal necessities before the Lord in prayer having perhaps each day 50 or more matters to bring before Him, and thus I obtain the blessing. I ask no human being for help concerning the work. No, if I could obtain £10,000 through each application for help; by God's grace, I would not ask. And why not? Because I have dedicated my whole life cheerfully to the precious service of giving to the world and to the Church, a clear, distinct, and undeniable demonstration, that it is a blessed thing to trust in and to wait upon God. That He is now, as He ever was, the Living God, the same as revealed in the Holy Scriptures, and if we know and are reconciled to Him through faith in the Lord Jesus and ask Him in His name for that which is according to His will, He will surely give it to us in His own time, if we believe that He will. "Nor has God failed me at any time. Forty years have I proved His faithfulness in this work."

IN THE LORD JEHOVAH IS EVERLASTING STRENGTH

Under date November 9, 1861, Mr. Müeller wrote:

"November 9. Saturday evening. When this week commenced on November 3, I received only £3 19s. by the first delivery. Shortly after there came in the course of my reading, through the Holy Scriptures, Isaiah 26:4, *'Trust ye in the Lord for ever; for in the Lord Jehovah is everlasting strength.'* I laid aside my Bible, fell on my knees, and prayed thus: I believe that there is everlasting strength in the Lord Jehovah, and I do trust in Him; help me, O Lord, for ever to trust in Thee. Be pleased to give me more means this day, and much this week, though only so little now has come in. That same day, November 3, I received £10 from Surbiton, £5 from a donor residing in Clifton, £2 from a Bristol donor, and in the course of the week altogether £457 came in; thus Jehovah again proved, that in Him is everlasting strength, and that He is worthy to be trusted.

'Dear believing reader, seek but in the same way to trust in the Lord, if you are not in the habit of doing so already, and you will find as I have found thousands of times, how blessed it is. But if the reader should be yet going on in carelessness about his soul, and therefore be without the knowledge of God and His dear Son, then the first and most important thing one has to do is to trust in the Lord Jesus for the salvation of his soul, that he may be reconciled to God and obtain the forgiveness of his sins."

JESUS CHRIST, THE SAME YESTERDAY, AND TODAY, AND FOREVER

"May 26, 1861. At the close of the period I find, that the total expenditure for all the various objects was £24,700 16s. 4d or £67 13s. 5¾d. per day, all the year round. During the coming year I expect the expenses to be considerably greater. But God, who has helped me these many years, will, I believe, help me in future also.

'You see, esteemed reader, how the Lord, in His faithful love helped us year after year. With every year the expenses increased, because the operations of the Institutions were further enlarged; but He never failed us. You may say, however, 'What would you do, if He should fail in helping you?' My reply is, that cannot be, as long as we trust in Him and do not live in sin. But if we were to forsake Him, the fountain of living waters, and to hew out to ourselves broken cisterns, which cannot hold water by trusting in an arm of flesh; or if we were to live in sin we would then have to call upon Him in vain, even though we professed still to trust in Him, according to that word: *'If I regard iniquity in my heart, the Lord will not hear me'* (Psalm 66:18).

'Before this, by God's grace, I have been enabled to continue to trust in Him alone; and also before this, though failing and weak in many ways, yet by God's grace I have been enabled to walk uprightly, hating sin and loving holiness, and longing after increased conformity to the Lord Jesus."

"October 21, 1868. As the days come, we make known our requests to Him for our outgoings have now been for several years at the rate of more than One Hundred Pounds each day; but though the expenses have been so great, He has never failed us. We have indeed, as to the outward appearance, like the 'Burning Bush in the Wilderness;' yet we have not been consumed. Moreover, we are full of trust in the Lord, and therefore of good courage, though we have before us the prospect that year by year our expenses will increase more and more. If all my beloved fellow disciples who seek to work for God would know the blessedness of looking truly to God alone, and trusting in Him alone, they would soon see how soul refreshing this way is and how entirely beyond disappointment as far as He is concerned.

'Earthly friends may alter their minds regarding the work in which we are engaged; but if indeed we work for God, whoever may alter His mind regarding our service, He will not. Earthly friends may lose their ability to help us, however much they desire so to do; but He remains throughout eternity the infinitely Rich One. Earthly friends may have their minds diverted to other objects after a time, and, as they cannot help everywhere as much as they may desire it, they may reluctantly have to discontinue to help us. But He is able, always, even though the requirements may be multiplied a million times to supply all that can possibly be needed, and does it with delight where His work is carried on and where He is confided in.

'Earthly friends may be removed by death, and thus we may lose their help, but He lives forever, He cannot die. In this latter point of view I have especially seen during the past 40 years in connection with this Institution the blessedness of trusting in the Living God alone. Not one nor two, nor even five nor ten, but many more, who once helped me much with their means, have been removed by death; but have the operations of the Institution been stopped on that account? No. And how did this come? Because I trusted in God, and in God alone."

THOROUGHLY PREPARED IN THE HEART FOR TRIALS OF FAITH

Under the date July 28, 1874, Mr. Müeller wrote:

"It has for months appeared to me, as if the Lord meant, by His dealings with us, to bring us back to that state of things, in which we were for more than ten years. In August, 1838, to April, 1849, when we had day by day, almost without interruption to look to Him for our daily supplies, and for a great part of the time from meal to meal.

'The difficulties appeared to me indeed very great, as the Institution is now twenty times larger than it was then and our purchases are to be made in a wholesale way. But at the same time I am comforted by the knowledge that God is aware of all this; and that if this way be for the glory of His name and for the good of His Church and the unconverted world, I am, by His grace, willing to go this way and to do it to the end of my course. The funds were thus fast expended; but God our infinitely rich Treasurer remains to us and it is this that gives me peace.

'Moreover, if it pleases Him with a work requiring about £44,000 a year to make me do again at the evening of my life what I did from August, 1838, to April, 1849, I am not only prepared for it, but I will gladly again pass through all these trials of faith with regard to means if He only might be glorified, and His Church and the world be benefited. Very often this last point has of late passed through my mind and I have placed myself in the position of having no means at all left. I have Two Thousand and One Hundred persons not only daily at the table, but with everything else to be provided for, and all funds gone. One hundred and eighty-nine Missionaries to be assisted and nothing whatever left. About one hundred schools with about nine thousand scholars in them to be entirely supported and no means for them in hand. About Four Million Tracts and Tens of Thousands of copies of the Holy Scriptures to be sent out yearly, and all the money expended. Invariably, however, with this probability before me, I have said to myself: 'God, who has raised up this work through me, God who has led me generally year after year to enlarge it, God who has supported this work now for more than forty years will still help and will not suffer me to be confounded. Because I rely upon Him and commit the whole work to Him. Therefore, He will provide me with what I need in the future even though I know not when the means are to come.' Thus I wrote in my journal on July 28th, 1874."

How God Answered His Faithful Servant

"The reader will now be interested in learning how we fared under these circumstances.

When I came home, last evening (July 27), I found letters had arrived that contained £193, among which there was one from a Missionary in Foreign lands who had been helped by the funds of this Institution. He had come into the possession of some money, by the death of a relative and sent £153 0s. 4d. for Foreign Missions. This morning, July 28, came in £24 more and when I met this afternoon with several of my helpers for prayer for means and various other matters such as spiritual blessing upon the various Objects of the Institution, more rain in this very dry season, and the health of our fellow laborers, etc., we had received since yesterday afternoon altogether £217. We thanked God for it, and asked for more. When the meeting for prayer was over, there was handed to me a letter from Scotland, containing £73 17s. 10d. and a paper with 13s. This was the immediate answer to prayer for more means."

"August 1, 1874. The income for this whole week since August. 5 has been £897 15s. 6½d."

"September 16, 1874. Just after having again prayed for the payment of legacies, which have been left, I had a legacy receipt sent for the payment of a legacy for £1,800."

"September 23, 1874. The income today was £5,365 13s. 6d. of which there was sent in one donation £5,327 7s. 6d. The Lord be praised!"

STRONG IN FAITH AND GIVING GLORY TO GOD

On March 27, 1881, Mr. Müeller found that no money remained in hand for the School, Bible, Missionary and Tract Funds. Nearly £1,400 had been spent for these Objects during the previous month. He writes:

"What was now to be done, dear reader, under these circumstances, when all the money for the above Objects was again gone? I reply, we did what we have done for 47 years, that is, we waited continually upon God. My dear fellow laborers in Bristol, and my dear wife and I in America, brought our necessities again and again before the Lord.

'Here in the United States, besides our habitual daily prayer for help, we had special seasons 4, 5, and 6 times a day additionally for pouring out our hearts before our

Heavenly Father, and making known our requests unto Him. Being assured that help would come, we have not waited upon the Lord in vain. This plan may be despised by some, ridiculed by others, and considered insufficient by a third class of persons; but under every trial and difficulty we find prayer and faith to be our universal remedy. After having experienced for half a century their efficacy, we purpose by God's help, to continue waiting upon Him, in order to show to an ungodly world, and a doubting Church that the Living God is still able and willing to answer prayer. It is the joy of His heart to listen to the supplications of His children. In Psalm 9:10, the Divine testimony regarding Jehovah is, *'They that know thy name will put their trust in Thee.'* We know Him, by His grace, and do therefore put our trust in Him'"

"April 27, 1881. On March 27th we had no means at all in hand for these Objects, as stated under that date. We have now been helped through one more month in answer to prayer, and have been supplied with all we needed though that amounted to nearly £1000, and have £23 8s. 6¼d. left."

"April 29, 1881. A servant of the Lord Jesus, who, constrained by the love of Christ, seeks to lay up treasure in heaven after having received a legacy of £532 14s. 5d. gave £500 of it for these Objects."

"July 28, 1881. The income for some time has only been enough to cover the third part of the expenses. Consequently, all we have for the support of the Orphans is nearly gone; and for the first four Objects of the Institution we have nothing at all in hand. The natural appearance now is that the work cannot be carried on. But I *believe* that the Lord will help both with means for the Orphans and also for the other Objects of the Institution, and that we shall not be confounded but encouraged that the work shall not need to be given up. I am fully expecting help and have written this to the glory of God, that it may be recorded hereafter for the encouragement of His children. The result will be seen. The above was written at 7. July 28, 1881. As yet we have the means to meet our expenses, and I expect that we shall not be confounded, though for seven years we have not been so poor."

EXPECTATIONS RECEIVED AND SEEN

"The result has indeed been seen, and will be seen. For more than 20 years since those words were written and Mr. Müeller had thus recorded his confidence in the Lord's help. God *has* sustained the work, and in May, 1902, there was a balance in hand of some thousands of pounds, notwithstanding that more than £500,000 had been received and expended since this entry was made in Mr. Müeller's journal on July 28, 1881."

FAITH AND PATIENCE GREATLY TRIED

During these 20 years faith and patience were at times greatly tried:

"August 15, 1881. The balance for the Orphans is now reduced to £332 12s. 7d. it is lower than it has been for more than twenty-five years. This sum we have in hand to meet the daily expenses in connection with 2,100 persons is only enough for the average outgoings of 4½ days. But our eyes are upon the Lord. I look to my heavenly Provider. The total income of today has been £28 5s. 2½d."

"August 22, 1881. Part of a legacy, left years ago of £1,000 was paid as the answer to many prayers."

"February 26, 1882. The balance in hand today for the Orphans is £97 10s. 7½d. that is £24 more than the average expenses of one single day."

"March 2, 1882. Our position now regarding the Orphan work is praying day by day 'Give us this day our daily bread'. For a considerable time we have had day by day to look to the Lord for the supply of our daily needs; but God has helped us thus far."

"April 20, 1882. When in the greatest need we received from Edinburgh £100 with this statement: 'The enclosed was intended as a legacy, but I have sent it in my lifetime.'"

"June 3, 1882. Received from Wottan-under-Edge £500. A glorious deliverance was this donation, and a precious earnest of what God would do further for us."

"October 21, 1882. Received from Wottan-under-Edge £1,000. God, in answer to our prayers, spoke to His dear child, and inclined his heart to send to us more than ever. Thus He also gives proof that during the previous year when we were so low in funds, it was only for the trial of our faith and patience, and not in anger; nor did He thereby mean to indicate that He would not help us anymore. For my own part, I expected further great help from God, and I have not been confounded."

"August 17, 1883. Our balance was reduced this afternoon to £10 2s. 7d. Think of this, dear reader! Day by day about 2,100 persons are to be provided for in the Orphan Institution and £10 2s and 7d. was all that was in hand to do this. You see that we are in the same position we were 46 years ago as to funds. God is our banker. In Him we trust, and on Him we draw by faith. This was Saturday. In the evening £30 was received. On Monday we received £129 further, but had to pay out £60. On Tuesday we received £295, but had to pay out £180. God is pleased to continually vary His mode of dealing with us, in order that we may not be tempted to trust in donors, or in circumstances, but in Him alone and to keep our eye fixed upon Him. This, by His grace, we are enabled to do, and our hearts are kept in peace."

TEN MONTHS LATER...
THE LARGEST LEGACY EVER RECEIVED

"Some ten months later, when the balance in hand was only £41 10s., a very little more than one-half of the average expenses for the Orphans for one day, and there were sanitary operations advisable to be carried out, the expenses of which would amount to upwards of £2,000. Mr. Müeller received a legacy of £11,034 6s. on June 7, 1884. This is the largest donation I have ever received at one time. This legacy had been more than six years in Chancery, and year after year its payment was expected, but remained unsettled by the Chancery Court. I kept on praying, however, and for six years prayed day by day that the money might be paid, believing that God in His own time (which is always the best), would help at last; for many legacies in Chancery I had prayed out of the Court, and the money was eventually paid. In the present case, too, after faith and patience had been sufficiently exercised, God granted this request likewise."

THE REPORT OF 1893

1893. In the Fifty-fourth Report of the Scriptural Knowledge Institution Mr. Müeller says:

"The readers of the last report will remember under what particular trials we entered upon the last financial year of the Institution, from May 26th, 1892, to May 26th, 1893. But we trusted in God and with unshaken confidence we looked to Him, and we expected that we would somehow or other be helped. While we went on in these circumstances my heart was habitually at peace being assured that all this was permitted by God, to prepare a blessing for thousands who would afterwards read the record of His dealings with us, during the year from May 26th, 1892, to May 26th,

1893. With reference to our dear fellow laborers, Mr. Wright and I have seen already how God has blessed them while passing through the trial."

"August 30, 1892. This evening while reading in the Psalms, I came to Psalm 81:10 and remembered the work of the Holy Spirit in my heart, when reading this verse on December 5, 1835. The effect that this had not only on leading me to found the greatest Orphan Institution in the world, but I thought also of the blessing which has since been brought to tens of thousands of believers and unbelievers all over the world. Putting aside the Bible, therefore, I fell on my knees and asked God that He would graciously be pleased to repeat His former kindness, and to supply me again more abundantly with means. Accordingly in less than half an hour, I received £50 from a Bristol Donor and from Redland a large quantity of fish, in addition to £97 already received today as the result of much prayer. By the last delivery, at 9 I received £5 more, and had thus £152 in all this day as the result of prayer."

"November 11. There came in today, by the first two deliveries, only about £8, but the Lord increased the income to more than £200 before the end of this day. I am never discouraged by very little only coming in, but say to myself, and also to my dear helpers, more prayer, more patience, and more exercise of faith will bring greater blessing; for thus I have invariably found it, since October, 1830, now 63 years ago, when I first began this life of entire dependence upon God for everything."

"March 1, 1893. The income during this week ending today, was £92 8s. 8¾d. for the Orphans, and £9 11s. 2d. for the other Objects, being about the sixth part of our weekly expenses; but now the great trial of our faith was nearly brought to a close, as will presently be seen."

"March 4, 1893. This very day God begins to answer

our prayers, as we have received a very good offer for the land we have to sell, even £1,000 per acre. The beginning of the day was darker as to outward appearances than ever: but we trusted in God for help. The first three deliveries of letters brought us only £4, and the remaining three brought us so little that the whole day's income was only £8 instead of £90, the amount we require every day to meet all our expenses. But God has now helped us. This evening we have been able to sell ten acres of land and two-fifths of an acre at £1,000 per acre and shall receive £10,405 altogether for the whole of one field. The contract was signed at 8 o'clock this evening."

MR. MÜELLER'S DEPARTURE TO BE WITH CHRIST

On the evening of Wednesday, March 9th, 1898, Mr. Müeller took part in the usual meeting for prayer held in the Orphan House Number 3. He retired at his usual hour to rest, and early on the following morning (the 10th of March) alone, in his bedroom, he breathed his last. Fulfilling in him what had long been with him a most joyous anticipation that *"to depart and to be with Christ is far better"* (Philippians 1:23).

March 14, 1898. This day Mr. Müeller's earthly remains were laid in the grave of his first and second wives, at Arno' Vale Cemetery. The attendant circumstances throughout were very remarkable and interesting to the Christian mind, chiefly as illustrating God's eternal principle, *"Them that honour Me I will honour"* (1 Samuel 2:30). The man who in life sought not his own glory became in death the one to whom all classes delighted to show respect and honor. From the masses of sympathizing spectators that lined the streets, the tearful eyes and the audible prayerful exclamations that escaped the lips of bystanders (many of them the poorest of the poor), as the orphans filed past following the hearse; from the suspension of all traffic in the principal streets, the tolling of muffled bells, and the flags at half-mast, and from the dense crowds in the cemetery that awaited the arrival of the funeral company, it seemed as if the whole city had spontaneously resolved to do honor to the man who had not lived for himself, but for the glory of God and the good of his fellows.

For some 21 months before Mr. Müller's death the trials of faith and patience were great. Mr. James Wright, Mr. Müller's successor, writes:

"He, who is pleased to sometimes teach His servants 'how to abound,' sees it best for them at other times 'to be instructed how to suffer need.' For many of the 64 years during which this work has been carried on, the former was our experience; we abounded and richly abounded, lately and especially during the last 2 or 3 years it has been the very reverse. Pressing need has been the rule; a balance in hand over and above our need was the rare exception. Yet we have never been forsaken."

"September 23, 1897. Residue of the legacy of the late G. J., Esq., £2,679 18s. 7d. This sum was received when we were in the deepest need; and after it had pleased the Lord to allow a very protracted trial of faith and patience; but see, beloved reader, He did not disappoint nor forsake us, as He never does those who really trust in Him. The joy of such a deliverance cannot be tasted without the experience of the previous trial."

"February 26, 1898. The following entry under this date is in Mr. Müller's own hand-writing:

"The income today, by the two first deliveries, was £7 15s. 11d. Day by day our great trial of faith and patience continues, and thus it has been, more or less, now, for 21 months, yet, by Thy grace, we are sustained."

"March 1, 1898. The following again is from a memorandum in Mr. Müller's own hand-writing, under this date:

"For about 21 months with scarcely the least intermission the trial of our faith and patience has continued. Now today, the Lord has refreshed our hearts. This afternoon there came in for the Lord's work £1,427 1s. 7d. as part payment of a legacy of the late Mrs. E. C. S. For 3 years and 10 months this money had been in the Irish Chancery Court. Hundreds of petitions had been brought before the Lord regarding it, and now at last, this portion of the total legacy has been received."

"Thus the Lord, in love and faithfulness, greatly refreshed the heart of His servant, only nine days before taking him home to be with Him."

APPENDIX A
FIVE CONDITIONS OF PREVAILING PRAYER

1. Entire dependence upon the merits and mediation of the Lord Jesus Christ, as the only ground of any claim for blessing. (See John 14:13-14, 15:16.)

2. Separation from all known sin. If we regard iniquity in our hearts, the Lord will not hear us, for it would be sanctioning sin. (See Psalm 66:18.)

3. Faith in God's Word of promise as confirmed by His oath. Not to believe Him is to make Him both a liar and a perjurer. (See Hebrews 11:6, 6:13-20.)

4. Asking in accordance with His will. Our motives must be godly: we must not seek any gift of God to consume it upon our lusts. (See 1 John 5:14, James 4:3.)

5. Importunity in supplication. There must be waiting on God and waiting for God, as the husbandman has long patience to wait for the harvest. (See James 5:7; Luke 18:1-8.)

APPENDIX B

THE CAREFUL AND CONSECUTIVE READING OF THE HOLY SCRIPTURES

Concerning this subject Mr. Müeller says: "I fell into the snare, into which so many young believers fall, the reading of religious books in preference to the Scriptures. I could no longer read French and German novels as I had formerly done to feed my carnal mind; but still I did not put into the room of those books the best of all books. I read tracts, missionary papers, sermons, and biographies of godly persons. The last kind of books I found more profitable than others, and had they been well selected, or had I not read too much of such writings, or had any of them tended particularly to endear the Scriptures to me, they might have done me much good."

"I never had been at any time in my life in the habit of reading the Holy Scriptures. When under fifteen years of age, I occasionally read a little of them at school. But afterwards God's precious book was entirely laid aside, so that I never read one single chapter of it, as far as I remember, until it pleased God to begin a work of grace in my heart. Now the Scriptural way of reasoning would have been: God himself has condescended to become an author, and I am ignorant about that precious book, which His Holy Spirit has caused to be written through the instrumentality of His servants. It contains that which I ought to know and the knowledge of which will lead me to true happiness. Therefore, I ought to read again and again this most precious book, this book of books, most earnestly, most prayerfully, with much meditation; and I ought to continue in this practice all the days of my life. For I was aware, though I read it but little, that I knew scarcely anything of it.

'But instead of acting thus, and being led by my ignorance of the Word of God to study it more, my difficulty in understanding it and the little enjoyment I had in it made me careless of reading it (for much prayerful reading of the Word, gives not merely more knowledge, but increases the delight we have in reading it); and so, like many believers, I preferred for the first four years of my divine life the works of uninspired men to the oracles of the living God. The consequence was that I remained a babe, both in knowledge and grace. In knowledge I say; for all true knowledge must be derived by the Spirit from the Word. And because I neglected the Word, I was so ignorant for nearly four years that I did not clearly know even the fundamental points of our holy faith.

'This lack of knowledge most sadly kept me back from walking steadily in the ways of God. For it is the truth that makes us free, (John 8:31, 32) by delivering us from the slavery of the lusts of the flesh, the lusts of the eyes, and the pride of life. The Word proves it. The experience of the saints proves it; and also my own experience most decidedly proves it. For when it pleased the Lord in August of 1829, to bring me really to the Scriptures, my life and walk became very different. And even though since that I have very much fallen short of what I might and ought to be, yet, by the grace of God, I have been enabled to live much nearer to Him than before.

'If any believers read this who prefer other books to the Holy Scriptures, and who enjoy the writings of men much more than the Word of God, may they be warned by my loss. I shall consider this book to have been the means of doing much good, should it please the Lord through its instrumentality to lead some of His people no longer to neglect the Holy Scriptures, but to give them that preference, which they have hitherto bestowed on the writings of men. My dislike to increase the number of books would have been sufficient to deter me from writing these pages if I had not been convinced that this is the only way in which the brethren at large may be benefited through my mistakes and errors, and be influenced by the hope in answer to my prayers. I pray the reading of my experience may be the means of leading them to value the Scriptures more highly, and to make them the rule of all their actions.

'If anyone should ask me, how he may read the Scriptures most profitably, I would advise him, that:

1. Above all he should seek to have it settled in his own mind that God alone, by His Spirit, can teach him, and therefore, because he will be asking God for blessings, it would be good for him to seek God's blessing prior to reading, and also while reading.

2. He should have it settled in his mind that although the Holy Spirit is the best and sufficient teacher, that this teacher does not always teach immediately when we desire it. Therefore, we may have to ask Him again and again for the explanation of certain passages but He will surely teach us if indeed we are seeking for light prayerfully, patiently, and with a view to the glory of God.

3. It is of immense importance for the understanding of the Word of God, to read with a plan, beginning each day where we previously left off reading a portion of the Old or New Testament. This is important:

    First, because it throws light upon the connection; and a different course, according to how one selects particular chapters will make it utterly impossible ever to understand much of the Scriptures.

    Second, while we are in the natural body, we need

a change even in spiritual things; and this change the Lord has graciously provided in the great variety which is to be found in His Word.

Third, it tends to bring glory to God; for the leaving out of some chapters here and there, is in essence saying that certain portions are better than others, or that there are certain parts of revealed truth unprofitable or unnecessary.

Fourth, by the blessings of God, it may keep us from erroneous views. For in reading thus regularly through the Scriptures we are led to see the meaning of the whole, and also kept from laying too much stress upon certain favorite views.

Fifth, the Scriptures contain the whole revealed will of God, and therefore we ought to seek to read from time to time through the whole of that revealed will. I fear there are many believers in our day who have not even once read through the whole of the Scriptures. Yet in a few months, by reading only a few chapters every day they might accomplish it.

Sixth, it is also of the greatest importance to meditate on what we read, so that perhaps a small portion or even all of what we have read will give us the opportunity to meditate upon it during the course of the day. A small portion of a book, or an epistle, or a gospel we go to regularly for meditation, may also be considered every day, without causing oneself to be brought into bondage by this plan."

"Learned commentaries I have found to fill the head with many notions and often also with the truth of God; but when the Spirit teaches through the instrumentality of prayer and meditation, the heart is affected. The former kind of knowledge generally puffs up, and is often renounced when another commentary gives a different opinion and is often found to be good for nothing when it is to be carried out into practice. The latter kind of knowledge by the teaching of the Holy Spirit generally humbles, gives joy, and leads us nearer to God. It is not easily reasoned away; and having been obtained from God, and having entered into the heart it becomes our own and is also generally carried out."

APPENDIX C
PROVING THE WILL OF GOD

It is very instructive and helpful to see the way in which Mr. Müeller proved the will of the Lord, when exercised in heart about the enlargement of the Orphan work, so that not only 300 but 1000 Orphans might be provided for.

"December 11, 1850. The special burden of my prayer, therefore, is that God would be pleased to teach me His will. My mind has also been especially pondering, how I could know His will satisfactorily concerning this particular. I am sure that I shall be taught. Therefore, I desire to wait patiently for the Lord's time when He shall be pleased to shine on my path concerning this point."

"December 26, 1850. Fifteen days have elapsed since I wrote the preceding paragraph. Every day since then I have continued to pray about this matter with a goodly measure of earnestness, and by the help of God. There has passed scarcely an hour during these days, in which, while awake, this matter has not been more or less before me.

'But all without even a shadow of excitement. I converse with no one about it. I have not even done so with my dear wife. From this I refrain still, and deal with God alone about the matter, in order that no outward influence and no outward excitement may keep me from attaining unto a clear discovery of His will. I have the fullest and most peaceful assurance, that He will clearly show me His will.

'This evening I had again an especially solemn season for prayer to seek to know the will of God. But while I continue to entreat and beseech the Lord that He would not allow me to be deluded in this business, I may say I have scarcely any doubt remaining on my mind as to what will be the answer, that being that I should go forward in this matter. As this, however, is one of the most momentous steps that I have ever taken, I judge that I cannot go about this matter with too much caution, prayerfulness, and deliberation. I am in no hurry about it. I could wait for years, by God's grace, were this His will before even taking one single step towards this thing, or even speaking to anyone about it.

'On the other hand, I would set to work tomorrow, were the Lord to bid me do so. This calmness of mind, this having no will of my own in the matter, this only wishing to please my Heavenly Father in it, this only seeking His and not my honor in it; and this state of heart I say, is the fullest assurance to me that my heart is not under a fleshly excitement and if I am helped to go on, I shall know the will of God to the full.

'But while I write thus I cannot but add at the same time, that I do crave the honor and the glorious privilege to be more and more used by the Lord. I have served Satan much in my younger years, and I desire now with all my might to serve God, during the remaining days of my earthly pilgrimage. I am forty-five years and three months old. Every day decreases the number of days that I have to stay on Earth. I therefore desire with all my might to work. There are vast multitudes of Orphans to be provided for.

'I desire that it may be more abundantly manifest that God is still the hearer and answerer of prayer, and that He is the living God now, as He ever was and ever will be, when He shall, simply in answer to prayer, have condescended to provide me with a house for 700 Orphans, and with means to support them. This last consideration is the most important point in my mind. The Lord's honor is the principal point with me in this whole matter; and because that is the case, if He would be more glorified by my not going forward in this business, I would by His grace, be perfectly content to give up all thoughts about another

Orphan House. Surely, in such a state of mind, obtained by the Holy Spirit, Thou, O my Heavenly Father, will not suffer Thy child to be mistaken, much less to be deluded! By the help of God I shall continue further, day by day, to wait upon Him in prayer concerning this thing, until He shall bid me act."

"January 2, 1851. A week ago I wrote the preceding paragraph. During this week I have still been helped, day by day, and more than once every day, to seek the guidance of the Lord about another Orphan House. The burden of my prayer has still been that He, in His great mercy, would keep me from making a mistake.

'During the last week the Book of Proverbs has come in the course of my Scripture reading, and my heart has been refreshed in reference to this subject by the following passages: *'Trust in the Lord with all thine heart; and lean not unto thine own understanding. In all thy ways acknowledge Him, and He shall direct thy paths'* (Proverbs 3:5-6). By the grace of God I do acknowledge the Lord in my ways, and in this thing in particular; I have therefore the comfortable assurance that He will direct my paths concerning this part of my service, as to whether I shall be occupied in it or not. Further: *'The integrity of the upright shall preserve them; but the perverseness of fools shall destroy them'* (Proverbs 11:3). By the grace of God I am upright in this business. My honest purpose is to get glory to God. Therefore I expect to be guided aright. Further: *'Commit thy works unto the Lord and thy thoughts shall be established'* (Proverbs 16:3). I do commit my works unto the Lord, and therefore expect that my thoughts will be established. My heart is more and more coming to a calm, quiet, and settled assurance that the Lord will condescend to use me yet further in the Orphan Work. Here, Lord, is Thy servant!"

Mr. Müeller wrote down eight reasons against and eight reasons for establishing another Orphan House for Seven Hundred Orphans. The following is his last reason for so doing:

"I am peaceful and happy spiritually in the prospect of enlarging the work as on former occasions when I had to do so. This weighs particularly with me as a reason for going forward. After all the calm, quiet, prayerful consideration of the subject for about eight weeks, I am peaceful and happy spiritually in the purpose of enlarging the field. This, after all the heart searching I have had, the daily prayer to be kept from delusion and mistake in this thing, and taking myself to the Word of God, would not be the case, I judge, had not the Lord purposed to condescend to use me more than ever in this service.

'I, therefore, on the ground of the objections answered, and these eight reasons *for* enlarging the work, come to the conclusion that it is the will of the blessed God, that His poor and most unworthy servant should yet more extensively serve Him in this work, which he is quite willing to do."

"May 24. From the time that I began to write down the thoughts of my mind in December 1850, until this day, ninety-two more Orphans have been applied for, in addition to the seventy-eight already waiting for admission before. But this number increases rapidly as the work becomes more and more known."

"On the ground of what has been recorded above, I purpose to go forward in this service, and to seek to build, to the praise and honor of the living God, another Orphan House large enough to accommodate seven hundred Orphans."

Appendix C

APPENDIX D

SCRIPTURE TEXTS THAT MOLDED THE LIFE AND MINISTRY OF GEORGE MÜELLER

Certain marked Scripture precepts and promises had such a singular influence upon this man of God, and so often proved the guides to his course, that they illustrate.

Psalm 119:105: *"Thy word is a lamp unto my feet, And a light unto my path."*

Those texts which, at the parting of the way. Became to him God's sign boards showing him the true direction are here given as nearly as may be in the order that they became so helpful to him. The study of them will prove a kind of spiritual biography outlining his career.

John 3:16: *"God so loved the world that He gave His only begotten Son, that whosoever believeth in Him should not perish, but have everlasting life."*

Jeremiah 17:5: *"Thus saith the Lord; Cursed be the man that trusteth in man, and maketh flesh his arm, and whose heart departeth from the Lord."*

Psalm 34:9: *"O fear the Lord, ye his saints: for there is no want to them that fear him."*

Matthew 6:33: *"Seek ye first the Kingdom of God and His righteousness; and all these things shall be added unto you."*

2 Timothy 3:15: *"The holy scriptures, which are able to make thee wise unto salvation."*

John 14:13-14: *"And whatsoever ye shall ask in my name, that will I do, that the Father may be glorified in the Son. If ye shall ask any thing in my name, I will do it."*

Matthew 6:25-34: *"Therefore I say unto you, Take no*

thought for your life, what ye shall eat, or what ye shall drink; nor yet for your body, what ye shall put on. Is not the life more than meat, and the body than raiment? Behold the fowls of the air: for they sow not, neither do they reap, nor gather into barns; yet your heavenly Father feedeth them. Are ye not much better than they? Which of you by taking thought can add one cubit unto his stature? And why take ye thought for raiment? Consider the lilies of the field, how they grow; they toil not, neither do they spin: And yet I say unto you, That even Solomon in all his glory was not arrayed like one of these.

Wherefore, if God so clothe the grass of the field, which to day is, and to morrow is cast into the oven, shall he not much more clothe you, O ye of little faith? Therefore take no thought, saying, What shall we eat? or, What shall we drink? or, Wherewithal shall we be clothed? (For after all these things do the Gentiles seek:) for your heavenly Father knoweth that ye have need of all these things. But seek ye first the kingdom of God, and his righteousness; and all these things shall be added unto you. Take therefore no thought for the morrow: for the morrow shall take thought for the things of itself. Sufficient unto the day is the evil thereof."

John 7:17: "*If any man will do his will, he shall know of the doctrine, whether it be of God, or whether I speak of myself.*"

John 8:31-32: "*If ye continue in my word, then are ye my disciples indeed; 32 And ye shall know the truth, and the truth shall make you free.*"

Acts 8:36-38: "*And the eunuch said, See, here is water: what doth hinder me to be baptized? And Philip said, If thou believest with all thine heart, thou mayest. And he answered and said, I believe that Jesus Christ is the Son of God. And they went down both into the water, both Philip and the eunuch, and he baptized him.*"

Romans 6: 3-4: "*Know ye not that so many of us as were baptized into Jesus Christ were baptized into His death? Therefore we are buried with Him by baptism into death.*"

Acts 20:7: "*Upon the first day of the week, when the disciples came together to break bread.*"

James 2:1-6: "*My brethren, have not the faith of our Lord Jesus Christ, the Lord of glory, with respect of persons. For if there come unto your assembly a man with a gold ring, in goodly apparel, and there come in also a poor man in vile raiment; And ye have respect to him that weareth the gay clothing, and say unto him, Sit thou here in a good place; and say to the poor, Stand thou there, or sit here under my footstool: Are ye not then partial in yourselves, and are become judges of evil thoughts? Hearken, my beloved brethren, Hath not God chosen the poor of this world rich in faith, and heirs of the kingdom which he hath promised to them that love him? But ye have despised the poor. Do not rich men oppress you, and draw you before the judgment seats?*"

Romans 7:6: "*Having, then, gifts differing according to the grace that is given us.*"

1 Corinthians 11:11: "*All these worketh that one and the selfsame Spirit, dividing to every man severally as he will.*"

Philippians 4:17: "*Not because I desire a gift: but I desire fruit that may abound to your account.*"

Matthew 6:25-32: "*Therefore I say unto you, Take no thought for your life, what ye shall eat, or what ye shall drink; nor yet for your body, what ye shall put on. Is not the life more than meat, and the body than raiment? Behold the fowls of the air: for they sow not, neither do they reap, nor gather into barns; yet your heavenly Father feedeth them. Are ye not much better than they? Which of you by taking thought can add one cubit unto his stature? And why take ye thought for raiment? Consider the lilies of the field, how they grow; they toil not, neither do they spin: And yet I say unto you, That even Solomon in all his glory was not arrayed like one of these. Wherefore, if God so clothe the grass of the field, which to day is, and to morrow is cast into the oven, shall he not much more clothe you, O ye of little faith? Therefore take no thought, saying, What shall we eat? or, What shall we drink? or, Wherewithal shall we be clothed? (For after all these things do the Gentiles seek:) for your heavenly Father knoweth that ye have need of all these things."*

Matthew 6:19: *"Lay not up for yourselves treasures upon earth."*

Luke 13:33: *"Sell that ye have and give alms."*

John 3:27: *"A man can receive nothing except it be given him from heaven."*

Psalm 66:18: *"If I regard iniquity in my heart, the Lord will not hear me."*

Psalm 4:3: *"Know that the Lord hath set apart him that is godly for Himself: The Lord will hear when I call unto Him."*

Genesis 22:14: *"Jehovah Jireh."* (The Lord will provide.)

Hebrews 13:5-6: *"He hath said, I will never leave thee, nor forsake thee; so that we may boldly say, the Lord is my helper."*

Proverbs 22:26: *"Be thou not one of them that strike hands, or of them that are sureties for debts."*

Proverbs 11:15: *"He that hateth suretyship is sure."*

2 Corinthians 11:15: *"I will very gladly spend and be spent for you; though the more abundantly I love you, the less I be loved."*

Galatians 3:26: *"Ye are all children of God by faith in Christ Jesus."*

1 Peter 1:7: *"Casting all your care upon Him for He careth for you."*

Philippians 4:6: *"Be careful for nothing, but in everything by prayer and supplication with thanksgiving let your requests be made known unto God."*

John 11:40: *"Said I not unto thee, that, if thou wouldest believe, thou shouldest see the glory of God?"*

Romans 8:28: *"We know that all things work together for good to them that love God."*

Genesis 18:25b: *"Shall not the judge of all the earth do right?"*

Matthew 19:14: *"Of such* [little children] *is the kingdom of heaven."*

Romans 8:32: *"He that spared not His own Son, but delivered Him up for us all, how shall He not with Him also freely give us all things?"*

James 1:17: *"Every good gift and every perfect gift is from above."*

Psalm 34:10: *"The young lions do lack and suffer hunger; but they that seek the Lord shall not want any good thing."*

Proverbs 11:24-25: *"There is that scattereth and yet increaseth; and there is that withholdeth more than is meet, but it tendeth to poverty. The liberal soul shall be made fat, and he that watereth shall be watered also himself."*

Luke 6:38: *"Give and it shall be given unto you: good measure, pressed down and shaken together, and running over, shall men give unto your bosom. For with the same measure that ye mete withal it shall be measured to you again."*

Isaiah 32:8: *"The liberal deviseth liberal things; and by liberal things shall he stand."*

Mark 14:7: *"For ye have the poor with you always, and whensoever ye will ye may do them good."*

Romans 14:16: *"Let not then you good be evil spoken of."*

Philippians 4:5: *"Let your moderation be known unto all men."*

James 1:2-4: *"My brethren, count it all joy when ye fall into divers temptations; knowind this, that the trying of your faith worketh patience. But let patience have her perfect work, that ye may be perfect and entire, wanting nothing."*

Proverbs 3:5-6: *"Trust in the Lord with all think heart; and lean not unto thine own understanding. In all thy ways acknowledge Him, and He shall direct thy paths."*

Proverbs 11:3: *"The integrity of the upright shall guide them; but the perverseness of transgressors shall destroy them."*

Proverbs 26:3: *"Commit thy works unto the Lord and thy thoughts shall be established."*

Romans 12:3: *"For I say, through the grace given unto me, to every man that is among you, not to think of himself more highly than he ought to think; but to think soberly, according as God hath dealt to every man the measure of faith."*

Psalm 27:14: *"Wait on the Lord; be of good courage, and he shall strengthen thine heart: Wait, I say, on the Lord."*

Hebrews 6:15: *"After he had patiently endured he obtained the promise."*

John 16:23: *"Verily, verily, I say unto you, Whatsoever ye shall ask the Father in my name, he will give it you."*

2 Corinthians 9:6: *"He which soweth sparingly shall reap also sparingly; and he which soweth bountifully shall also reap bountifully.*

1 Corinthians 6:20: *"Ye are bought with a price: therefore glorify God in your body, and in your spirit, which are God's."*

Psalm 9:10: *"And they that know thy name will put their trust in thee: for thou, LORD, hast not forsaken them that seek thee."*

Isaiah 26:3-4: *"Thou wilt keep him in perfect peace, whose mind is stayed on thee: because he trusteth in thee.*

Trust ye in the Lord for ever: for in the Lord Jehovah is everlasting strength."

2 Corinthians 8:12: *"If there be first a willing mind it is accepted according to that a man hath and not according to that he hath not."*

1 Corinthians 15:58: *"Therefore, my beloved brethren, be ye stedfast, unmoveable, always abounding in the work of the Lord, forasmuch as ye know that your labour is not in vain in the Lord."*

Galatians 6:9: *"Let us not be weary in well doing, for in due season we shall reap if we faint not."*

Psalm 31:19: *"Oh how great is thy goodness, which thou hast laid up for them that fear thee; which thou hast wrought for them that trust in thee before the sons of men!"*

Psalm 119:68: *"Thou art good and doest good."*

Psalm 119:75: *"I know, O LORD, that thy judgments are right, and that thou in faithfulness hast afflicted me."*

Psalm 31:15: *"My times are in Thy Hand."*

Psalm 84:11: *"For the Lord God is a sun and shield: the Lord will give grace and glory: no good thing will he withhold from them that walk uprightly."*

Psalm 119:117: *"Hold Thou me up and I shall be safe."*

Revelation 22:12: *"Behold I come quickly, and My reward is with Me, to give every man according as his work shall be."*

Matthew 6:11: *"Give us this day our daily bread."*

Ephesians 3:20: *"Now unto Him that is able to do exceeding abundantly above all we ask or think."*

1 Samuel 2:30b: *"Them that honour Me I will honour."*

1 Peter 1:7: *"That the trial of your faith, being much more precious than of gold that perisheth, though it be tried with fire, might be found unto praise and honour and glory at the appearing of Jesus Christ."*

ANSWERS TO PRAYER

Appendix E

Apprehension of Truth

The Word of God Alone is our Standard

1. That the Word of God alone is our standard of judgment in spiritual things; that it can be explained only by the Holy spirit; and that in our day as well as in former times He is the teacher of His people. The office of the Holy Spirit I had not experimentally understood before that time. Indeed, of the office of each of the blessed persons commonly called the Trinity, I had not experimental apprehension.

I had not seen from the Scriptures that the Father chose us before the foundation of the world, and that in Him the wonderful plan of redemption originated. Also that He appointed all the means by which it was to be brought about. Further, that the Son in order to save us had to fulfill the law by satisfying its demands and with it the holiness of God by bearing the punishment due to our sins to satisfy the justice of God. Furthermore, that the Holy Spirit alone can teach us about our state by nature, show us the need of a Savior, enable us to believe in Christ, explain the Scriptures, and help us in preaching.

It was my beginning to understand this latter point in particular that had a great effect on me; for the Lord enabled me to put it to the test of experience by laying aside commentaries and almost every other book and reading the Word of God and studying it.

The result was that the first evening I shut myself in my room to give myself to prayer and meditation on the Scriptures: I learned more in a few hours than I had done during months previously. But the particular difference was that I receive real strength for my soul in doing so. I now began to try to test the Scriptures on things I had learned and seen and I found that only those principles that stood the test were of any value.

2. Before this time I had been much opposed to the doctrines of election, redemption in particular, and final persevering grace so much so that a few days after arriving at Teignmouth I called election a devilish doctrine. I did not believe that I had brought myself to the Lord, for that was manifestly false; but yet I held the opinion that I might have resisted finally. Furthermore, I knew nothing about the choice of God's people and did not believe that a child of God when once made safe by the Lord was safe forever. In my fleshly mind I had repeatedly said if I once I could prove that I am a child of God forever, I might go back in the world for a year to two and return to the Lord, and at last be saved. But now I was brought to examine these precious truths by the Word of God. Being made willing to have no glory of my own in the conversion of sinners, but to consider myself merely as an instrument; and being made willing to receive what the Scriptures said, I went to the Word, and read the New Testament from the beginning with particular reference to these truths. To my great astonishment I found that the passages that speak decidedly for election and persevering grace were

about four times as many as those that speak against the truths. Even those few I shortly afterward found when I had examined them and understood them served to confirm me in the above doctrines.

As to the effect that my belief in these doctrines had on me, I am constrained to state that though I am still exceedingly weak and by no means so dead to the lusts of the flesh, the lust of the eyes, and the pride of life as I ought to be, yet, by the grace of God, I have walked more closely with Him since that period. My life has not been so variable and I have lived much more for God than before. I have been strengthened by the Lord in great measure through these truths. For in the time of temptation I have been repeatedly led to say: Should I thus sin? I would only bring misery to into my soul for a time and dishonor God; for as a son of God forever I would have to be brought back again, though it might be in the way of severe chastisement. Therefore, I say the electing love of God in Christ has often been the means of producing holiness, instead of leading me into sin. It is only the notional apprehension of such truths, by that I mean, the desire to have them in the heart while they are still in the head that is dangerous.

3. Another truth, into which in a measure I was led, was in the Lord's coming. My views concerning this point up to that time had been completely vague and unscriptural. I had believed what others told me without checking it in the Word. I thought that things were getting better and better and that soon the whole world would be converted. But now I found in the Word of God that we have not

the least scriptural warrant to look for the conversion of the world before the return of the Lord. I found in the Scriptures, that which will usher in the glory of the Church and uninterrupted joy of the saints is the return of the Lord Jesus, and until then things will be more or less in confusion. I found in the Word that the return of Jesus, and not death, was the hope of the apostolic Christians; and that it would be wise for me, therefore, to look for His appearing. This truth entered so strongly in my heart that though I went into Devonshire exceedingly weak, I no longer looked for death, but was made to look for the return of the Lord. Having seen this truth, the Lord also graciously enabled me to apply it to my own heart and put the solemn question to myself. What may I do for the Lord before He returns as He may soon come?

4. In addition to these truths the Lord led me to see a higher standard of devotedness than I had seen before. He led me to see what my true glory in this world should be. To be despised, and to be poor by Christ's example. I saw then though I have seen it more fully since, that it ill becomes the servant to seek to be rich, great, and honored in the world where his Lord was poor and despised.

Appendix F

Arguments in Prayer for the Orphan Work

The Arguments That I Plead With God Are:

1. That I set about the work for the glory of God, that there might be visible proof by God supplying in answer to prayer only, the necessities of the orphans. That He is the living God and most willing to answer prayer, and that, therefore, He would be pleased to send supplies.

2. That God is the "Father of the fatherless," and that He, therefore, as their Father would be pleased to provide.

3. That I have received the children in the name of Jesus and therefore, He, in these children, has been received, and is fed, and is clothed, and therefore, He would be pleased to consider this.

4. That the faith of many of the children of God has been strengthened by this work, and that if God were to withhold the means for the future those who are weak in faith would be staggered, while by a continuance of means their faith might continue to be strengthened.

5. That many enemies would laugh if the Lord were to withhold supplies and they would say, did we not foretell that this enthusiasm would come to nothing?

6. That many children of God who are uninstructed or in a carnal state would be themselves justified to

continue their alliance with the world in the work of God and continue in their unscriptural proceeding respecting similar institutions as far as means is concerned if God were not to help me.

7. That the Lord would remember that I am His child, and that He would graciously pity me and remember that I cannot provide for these children. Therefore, He would not allow this burden to lie upon me long without sending help.

8. That He would remember likewise my fellow laborers in the work who trust in Him. But who would be tried were He to withhold supplies.

9. That He would remember that I would have to dismiss the children from under scriptural instruction to their former companions.

10. That He would show that those were mistaken who said, that in the beginning supplies might be expected while things were new, however, not afterwards.

11. That I would not know if He were to withhold means what explanation I would give upon the many most remarkable answers to prayer that He has given me before in the connection with this work and which most fully have shown to me that it is of God.

APPENDIX G

THE WISE SAYINGS OF GEORGE MÜELLER

THE BODY

CARE OF THE BODY.

I find it a difficult thing while caring for this body not to neglect the soul. It seems to me much easier to go on altogether regardless of the body, in the service of the Lord, than to take care of the body in the time of sickness and not to neglect the soul, especially in an affliction like my present one when the head allows but little reading or thinking. What a blessed prospect to be delivered from this wretched evil nature!

HABITS OF SLEEP

My own experience has been, almost invariably, that if I have not the needful sleep, my spiritual enjoyment and strength is greatly affected by it. I judge it of great benefit that the believer while traveling should seek as much as possible to refrain from traveling by night, or from traveling in such a way as that he is deprived of the needful night's rest. For without renewed bodily and mental strength to give him to prayer and meditation and the reading of the holy Scriptures, he will feel the pernicious effects of this all day long. There may be cases when traveling by night cannot be avoided, but if it can, even if we have to lose time by it and it might cost more money, I would affectionately and solemnly recommend refraining from night travel. In addition to our drawing beyond measure upon our bodily strength, we might also lose spiritually. The next thing I would advise with reference to travel is to take time morning by morning before setting out for meditation and prayer and reading of the Word of God. For although we are always exposed to temptation we are especially exposed during travel. Seek to ascertain the mind of God before you go on a journey to be quite sure it is His will that you go, lest you needlessly expose yourself to one of those special opportunities of the devil to ensnare you.

CHILDREN

CONVERSION OF CHILDREN

As far as my experience goes, it appears to me that believers generally have expected far too little of present fruit upon their labor among children. There has been a hoping that the Lord some day or other give their children instruction. In the Scriptures such as Proverbs 22:6 and many others we are instructed to bring up the children in the admonition of the Lord and that the salvation of their little souls is a very present need. I add as an encouragement to believers who labor among children that during the last two years, seventeen other young persons or children from the age of eleven to seventeen have received salvation and received into the fellowship among us, and that I am now looking for many more to be converted and that not merely of the orphans, but of the Sunday and Day School children.

NEGLECT OF CHILDREN

The power for good or evil that resides in a little child is great beyond all human calculation. A child rightly trained may be a world-wide blessing, with an influence reaching onward to eternal years. But a neglected or misdirected child may live to blight and blast mankind and leave influences of evil that will roll on in increasing volume until they plunge into the gulf of eternal perdition.

A remarkable instance was related by Dr. Harris,

of New York, at a recent meeting of the State Charities Aid Association. "In a small village in a county on the upper Hudson, some seventy years ago, a young girl named Margaret was sent adrift on the casual charity of the inhabitants. She became the mother of a long race of criminals and paupers. Her progeny has cursed the county ever since. The county records show two hundred of her descendants who have become criminals. In one single generation of her unhappy line there were twenty children; of these, three died in infancy, and seventeen survived to maturity. Of the seventeen, nine served in the State prison for high crimes an aggregate term of fifty years, while the others were frequent inmates of jails and penitentiaries and almshouses. Of the nine hundred descendants, through six generations, from this unhappy girl who was left on the village streets and abandoned in her childhood, a great number have been idiots, imbeciles, drunkards, lunatics, paupers, and prostitutes: but two hundred of the more vigorous are on record as criminals. This neglected little child has thus cost the county authorities, in the effects she has transmitted, hundreds of thousands of dollars in the expense and care of criminals and paupers beside the untold damage she has inflicted on property and public morals."

TRAINING OF CHILDREN

Seek to instill in your children the habit of being interested in the work of God, and about cases of need and distress at suitable times and under suitable circumstances and you will reap fruit from so doing.

CHRISTIAN LIFE

BEGINNING OF LIFE

God alone can give spiritual life at the first, and keep it up in the soul afterwards.

CROSS-BEARING

The Christian, like the bee, might suck honey out of every flower. I saw upon a snuffer stand in bas relief, "A heart, a cross under it, and roses under both." The meaning was obviously this that the heart that bears the cross for a time meets with roses afterwards.

KEEPING PROMISES

It has been often mentioned to me that brethren in business do not sufficiently attend to the keeping of promises. I cannot, therefore but urge all who love our Lord Jesus, who are engaged in a trade or business to seek for His sake not to make any promises, except those they shall be able to fulfill. Weigh all circumstances carefully before making any promises lest they should fail in accomplishment. It is even in these little affairs of life that we may either bring much honor or dishonor to the Lord. Why should it be so often said: Believers are bad servants, bad tradesman, and bad masters?" Surely it ought not to be true that we, who have power with God to obtain by prayer and faith all needful grace, wisdom, and skill, should be bad servants, bad tradesmen, and bad masters.

THE LOT AND THE LOTTERY

It is altogether wrong that I, as child of God, should have anything to do with so worldly a system as that of the lottery. But it was also unscriptural to go to the lot at all for the sake of ascertaining the Lord's mind, and this I ground on the following reasons. We have neither a commandment of God for it, nor the example of our Lord, nor that of the apostles after the Holy Spirit had been given on the Day of Pentecost.

We have many exhortations in the Word of god to seek to know His mind by prayer and searching of the Scriptures, but no passage that exhorts us to use the lot. The example of the apostles (Acts 1) in using the lot in the choice of an apostle in the place of Judas Iscariot, is the only passage that can be brought in favor of the lot from the New Testament (and to the Old we have not to go under this dispensation for the sake of finding how we ought to live as disciples of Christ). Now concerning this circumstance we have to remember that the Spirit was not yet given, by whose teaching it is that we know the mind of the Lord by prayer and fasting.

OBEDIENCE

Every instance of obedience from right motives strengthens us spiritually, while every act of disobedience weakens us spiritually.

SEPARATION UNTO GOD

May the Lord grant that the eyes of many of His children may be opened so they may seek in all spiritual things to be separated from unbelievers and to do God's work according to God's mind!

SERVICE TO ONE'S GENERATION

My business is to serve my own generation with all my might, and in so doing, I shall best serve the next generation, should the Lord tarry....The longer I live, the more I am enabled to realize that I have but one life for sowing in comparison with eternity for reaping.

SURETY FOR DEBT

How precious it is to act according to the Word of God! This perfect revelation of His mind gives us directions for everything, even the most minute affairs of this life. It commands us, "Be thou not one of them that strike hands, or of them that are sureties for debts." The way in which Satan ensnares persons to bring them into his het and to trouble them by becoming sureties is that he seeks to represent the matter as if there were no danger connected with a particular case which is not true. The Lord, the faithful Friend, tells us in His own Word that the only way in such a matter to be sure is to hate suretyship.

Helping One Another

As to the importance of the children of God opening their hearts to each other, especially when they are getting into a cold state, or under the power of a certain sin, or in special difficulty. I know from my own experience how often the snare of the devil has been broken when under the power of sin, how often the heart has been comforted when nigh to being overwhelmed. And how often advice has been obtained during great perplexity by opening my heart to a brother whom I had confidence. We are children of the same family and therefore ought to be helpers of each other.

Pastoral Visitation

An unvisited church will sooner or later become an unhealthy church.

Faith

Where Faith begins, anxiety ends; where anxiety begins, Faith ends.

Ponder these words of the Lord Jesus, "Only believe." As long as we are able to trust in God, holding fast in heart, that He is able and willing to help those who rest on the Lord Jesus for salvation, in all matters that are for His glory and their good, the heart remains calm and peaceful. It is only when we let go of faith in His power or His love that we lose our peace and become troubled. This very day I am in great trial in connection with the work in which I am engaged; yet my soul was calmed and quieted by the remembrance of God's power and love. I said to myself this morning: "As David encouraged himself in Jehovah his

God when he returned to Ziklag, so will I encourage myself in God;" and the result was peace of soul....The greater the difficulties, the easier for faith. As long as there remain certain natural prospect, faith does not get on as easily as when all natural prospect fail.

DEPENDENCE ON GOD

'Observe two things. We acted for God in delaying the public meetings and the publishing of the Report; but God's way lead always into trial, so far as sight and sense are concerned. Nature will always be tried in God's ways. The Lord was saying by this poverty, "I will now see whether you truly lean upon me, and whether you truly look to me." Of all the seasons that I have even passed through since I had been living this way, I never knew any period in which my faith was tried so sharply as during the four months from December 12, 1841 to April 12, 1842.

'But observe further, we could have altered our minds with respect to the public meetings and publishing the Report; for no one knew our determination concerning this point. However, on the contrary, we knew with what delight very many children of God were looking forward to receive further accounts. But the Lord kept us steadfast to the conclusion at which we arrived under His guidance.

GIFT AND GRACE OF FAITH

It pleased the Lord I think to give me in some cases something like the gift (not grace) of faith, so that unconditionally I could ask and look for an answer. The difference between the gift and the grace of faith seems to be this. According to the gift of faith I am able to do a thing, or believe that a thing will come to pass. The not doing of which, or the not believing of which would not be sin. According to the grace of faith I am able to do a thing, or believe that a thing will come to pass, if I have the

Word of God as the ground to rest upon, and, therefore, the not doing it, or the not believing it would be sin. For instance, the gift of faith would be needed, to believe that a sick person would be restored again, though there is no human probability: for there is no promise to that effect; the grace of faith is needed to believe that the Lord will give me the necessaries of life, if I first seek the Kingdom of God and His righteousness: for there is a promise to that effect. Matthew 6:33.

SELF-WILL

The natural mind is ever prone to reason, when we ought to believe; to be at work when we ought to be quiet; to go our own way, when we ought to steadily walk on in God's ways, however trying the nature.

TRIALS OF FAITH

The Lord gives faith, for the very purpose of trying it for the glory of His own name, and for the good of him who has it; and by the very trial of our faith we not only obtain blessing to our own souls by becoming the better acquainted with God, if we hold fast our confidence in Him. But our faith is also, strengthened by the exercise and so it becomes that if we walk with God in any measure of uprightness of heart the trials of faith will be greater and greater.

It is for the church's benefit that we are put in these straits; and if in the hour of need we were to take goods on credit, the first and primary object of the work would be completely frustrated and no heart would be strengthened to trust in God. Nor would there be any longer that manifestation of the special and particular providence of God, which has hitherto been so abundantly shown through this work, so that in the eyes of unbelievers they have been led to see that there is reality in the things of God, and many through these printed accounts have been truly converted. For these reasons, then, we consider it our precious privilege to continue to wait upon the Lord only, instead of taking goods on credit, or borrowing money from some kind friends, when we are in need. Nay, we purpose, as God shall give us grace, to look to Him only.

Even though morning after morning we have nothing in hand for the work, yes, and even though from meal to meal we have to look to Him. Because we are fully assured that He who is now (1845) in the tenth year feeding these many orphans and who has never suffered them to want, and that He who is now (1845) in the twelfth year of carrying on the other parts of the work without any branch of having had to be stopped for want of means, will do so for the future also. And here I do desire in the deep consciousness of my natural helplessness and dependence upon the Lord to confess that through the grace of God my soul has been in peace, though day by day we have had to wait for our daily provision upon the Lord; yes, though even from meal to meal we have been required to do this.

GIVING

ASKING GIFTS, ETC.

It is not enough to obtain means for the work of God, but these means should be obtained in God's way. To ask unbelievers for means is not God's way; to *press* even believers to give, is *not* God's way; but the *duty* and the *privilege* of being allowed to contribute to the work of God should be pointed out, and this should be followed up with earnest prayer, believing prayer, and will result in the desired end.

CLAIMS OF GOD

It is true, the Gospel demands our all; but I fear that in the general claim on all, we have shortened the claim on everything. We are not under law. True; but that is not to make our obedience less complete, or our giving less bountiful. But isn't it true that after all the claims of law are settled the new nature finds its joy in doing more than the law requires? Let us abound in the work of the Lord more and more.

GIVING IN ADVERSITY

At the end of the last century a very godly and liberal merchant in London was one day called on by a gentleman to ask him for some money for a charitable object. The gentleman expected very little, having just heard that the merchant had sustained heavy loss from the wreck of some of his ships. However, contrary to expectation, he received about ten times as much as he had expected for his object. He was unable to refrain from expressing his surprise to the merchant and told him what he had heard about the shipwreck of his vessels and how he feared he would scarcely have received anything. He then asked whether there was a mistake about the shipwreck of the vessels. The merchant replied,

"It is quite true, I have sustained heavy loss by these vessels being wrecked, but that is the very reason why I give you so much; for I must make better use than ever of my stewardship lest it should be entirely taken from me."

How should we act if prosperity in our business, our trade, our profession, etc., would suddenly cease, notwithstanding our having given a considerable proportion of our means for the Lord's work? My reply is this: "In the day of adversity *consider.*" Is it the will of God that we should ponder our ways; that we should see whether there is any particular reason, why God has allowed this to befall us. In doing so, we may find that we have looked too much on our prosperity as a matter of course, and have not sufficiently recognized the hand of God in our success.

'Or it may be, while the Lord has been pleased to prosper us, we have spent too much on ourselves, and may have thus, though unintentionally, *abused* the blessing of God. I do not mean by this remark to bring any children of God into bondage, so that with a scrupulous conscience they should look at every penny that they spend on themselves. This is not the will of God concerning us; and yet, on the other hand, there is truly such a thing as propriety or impropriety in our dress, our furniture, our table, our house, our establishment, and in the yearly amount we spend on ourselves and family.

GIVING AND HOARDING

I have every reason to believe that had I begun to lay up the Lord would have stopped the supplies, and thus the ability of doing so was only *apparent*. Let no one profess to trust in God, and yet lay up for future wants, otherwise the Lord will first send him to the hoard he has amassed, before He can answer the prayer for more. "There is that scattereth, and yet increaseth; and there is that withholdeth more than is meet, but it tendeth to poverty" (Proverbs 11:24). Notice here the word *"more than is meet;"* it is not said, withholdeth all; but *"more than is meet,"* while he gives, it is so little, in comparison with what it might be, and ought to be, that it tendeth to poverty.

MOTIVES IN GIVING

Believers should seek more and more to enter into the grace and love of God in giving His only begotten Son, and into the grace and love of the Lord Jesus, in giving himself in our place, so that by love and gratitude they may be increasingly led to surrender their bodily and mental strength, time, gifts, talents, property, position in life, rank, all they have and are to the Lord.

By this I do not mean, that they should give up their business, trade, or profession, and become preachers for the Lord. Nor do I mean that they should take all their money and give it to the first beggar who asks for it. But they should hold all they have and are for the Lord, not as owners but as stewards, and be willing to use part or all they have *at His bidding*. However short the believer may fall, nothing less than this should be his aim.

STEWARDSHIP

It is the Lord's order that He is pleased to make us His stewards in every way. For whether in temporal or spiritual things, if we are indeed acting as *stewards* and not as *owners,* He will make us stewards over *more.*

Even in this life as to temporal things, the Lord is pleased to repay those who act for Him as stewards, and who contribute to His work or to the poor, as He may be pleased to prosper them. But how much greater is the *spiritual* blessing we receive, both in this life and in the world to come, if constrained by the love of Christ, we act as God's stewards with that which He is pleased to entrust us!

SYSTEMATIC GIVING

Only *fix even the smallest amount* you purpose to give of your income, and give this regularly; and as God is pleased to increase your light and grace, and is pleased to prosper you more, so give more. If you neglect *habitual giving, regular giving, or giving from principle and upon scriptural ground* and leave it only to feeling and impulse, or particular arousing circumstances, you will certainly be a loser.

A merchant in the United States said in answer to inquiries relative to his mode of giving:

"In consecrating my life anew to God, and aware of the ensnaring influence of riches and the necessity of deciding on a plan of charity before wealth should bias my judgment, I adopted the following system:

'I decided to balance my accounts as nearly as I could every month, reserving such portion of profits as might appear adequate to cover probable losses, and to lay aside, by entry on a benevolent account, one tenth of the remaining profits, great or small, as a fund for benevolent expenditure, supporting myself and family on the remaining nine tenths. I further determined that if at any time my net profits, that is profits from which clerk hire and store expenses had been deducted, should exceed five hundred dollars in a month, I would give 12½ per cent.; if over seven hundred dollars, 15 per cent.; if over nine hundred dollars, 17½ per cent.; if over thirteen hundred dollars, 22½ per cent,. Thus increasing the proportion of the whole as God should prosper me until at fifteen hundred dollars I would give 25 per cent, or 375 dollars a month. As capital was of the utmost importance to my success in business, I decided not to increase the foregoing scale until I had acquired a certain capital, after which I would give one quarter of all net profits, great or small. And on the acquisition of another certain amount of capital, I decided to give half, and on acquiring what I determined would be a full sufficiency of capital, then to give the whole of my net profits.

'It is now several years since I adopted this plan, and under it I have acquired a handsome capital, and have been prospered beyond my most sanguine expectations. Although constantly giving, I have never yet touched the bottom of my fund, and have repeatedly been surprised to find what large drafts it would bear. True, during some months, I have encountered a salutary trial of faith, when this rule has led me to lay by the tenth while the remainder proved inadequate to my support; but the tide has soon turned, and with gratitude I have recognized a heavenly hand more than making good all past deficiencies.'"

The following deeply interesting particulars are recorded in the memoir of Mr. Cobb, a Boston merchant. At the age of twenty-three, Mr. Cobb drew up and subscribed the following remarkable document:

"By the grace of God I will never be worth more than 50,000 dollars. By the grace of God I will give one fourth of the net profits of my business to charitable and religious uses. If I am ever worth 20,000 dollars I will give one half of my net profits; and if ever I am worth 30,000 dollars, I will give three fourths; and the whole after 50,000 dollars. So help me God, or give to a more faithful steward, and set me aside."

"To this covenant," says his memoir, "he adhered with conscientious fidelity." He distributed the profits of his business with an increasing ratio, from year to year, until he reached the point which he had fixed as a limit to his property, and then gave to the cause of God all the money which he earned. At one time, finding that his property had increased beyond 50,000 dollars, he at once devoted the surplus 7,500 dollars.

"On his death-bed he said, 'by the grace of God—nothing else—by the grace of God I have been enabled, under the influence of these resolutions to give away more than 40,000 dollars. How good the Lord has been to me!'" Mr. Cobb was also an active, humble, and devoted Christian, seeking the prosperity of feeble churches; laboring to promote the benevolent institutions of the day; punctual in his attendance at prayer meetings, and anxious to aid the inquiring sinner. He was watchful for the eternal interests of those under his charge; mild and amiable in his deportment; and, in the general tenor of his life and character an example of consistent piety. His last sickness and death were peaceful, and triumphant.

"It is a glorious thing," said he, "to die. I have been active and busy in the world. I have enjoyed life as much as anyone. God has prospered me. I have everything to bind me here. I am happy in my family. I have property enough, but how small and mean does this world appear on a sickbed! Nothing can equal my enjoyment in the near view of heaven. *My hope in Christ* is worth infinitely more than all other things. The blood of Christ, the blood of Christ, none but Christ! Oh! how thankful I feel that God has provided a way that I may look forward with joy to another world through His dear Son."

GOD

APPROVAL OF GOD

In the whole work we desire to stand with God, and not to depend upon the favorable or unfavorable judgment of the multitude.

CHASTISEMENTS OF GOD

Our Heavenly Father never takes any earthly thing from His children except He means to give them something better instead. The Lord, in His very love and faithfulness will not, and cannot, let us go on in backsliding but He will visit us with stripes, to bring us back to himself! The Lord never lays more on us, in the way of chastisement, than our state of heart makes needful; so that while He smites with the one hand, He supports with the other.

If, as believers in the Lord. Jesus, we see that our Heavenly Father, on account of wrong steps, or a wrong state of heart, is dealing with us in the way of discipline or correction, we have to be grateful for it. For He is acting towards us according to that selfsame love that led Him not to spare His only begotten Son, but to deliver Him up for us; and our gratitude to Him is to be expressed in words, and even by deeds. We have to guard against despising the chastening of the Lord, though we may not do so in word, and against *fainting* under chastisement: since all is intended for blessing to us.

FAITHFULNESS OF GOD

Perhaps you have said in your heart: "How would it be; suppose the funds of the orphans were reduced to nothing, and those who are engaged in the work had nothing of their own to give, and a mealtime were to come, and you had no food for the children?"

'Thus indeed it may be, for our hearts are desperately wicked. If ever we would be so left to ourselves that we depend no more upon the living God, or that "we regard iniquity in our hearts," then such a state of things, we have reason to believe, would occur. But so long as we shall are enabled to trust in the Living God, and though we fall short in every way of what we might be, and ought to be, we are at least kept from living in sin, such a state of things cannot occur.

'The Lord, to show His continued care over us, raises up new helpers. They that trust in the Lord shall never be confounded! Some who helped for a while may fall asleep in Jesus; others may grow cold in the service of the Lord; others may be as desirous as ever to help, but have no longer the means; others may have both a willing heart to help, and have also the means, but may see it the Lord's will to lay them out in another way. Therefore, if from one cause or another, were we to lean upon man, we would surely be confounded; but, in leaning upon the living God alone, we are *beyond disappointment, and* beyond *being forsaken because of death,* or *want of means,* or *want of love,* or *because of the claims of other work.* How precious to have learned in any measure to stand with God alone in the world, to be happy, and to know that surely no good thing shall be withheld from us while we walk uprightly!

PARTNERSHIP WITH GOD

A brother, who is in about the same state in which he was eight years ago, has very little enjoyment, and makes no progress in the things of God. The reason is that against his conscience he remains in a calling, which is opposed to the profession of a believer. We are exhorted in Scripture to abide in our calling; but only if we can abide in it *"with God"* (1 Corinthians 7:24).

POWER OF GOD

There is a worldly proverb, dear Christian reader, with which we are all familiar:"Where there is a will there is a way." If this is the proverb of those who know not God, how much more should believers in the Lord Jesus, who have power with God, say: Where there is a will there is a way."

TRUST IN GOD

Only let it be trust *in God,* not *in man,* not *in circumstances,* not *in any of your own exertions* but real trust in God, and you will be helped in your various necessities. Not in circumstances, not in natural prospects, not in former donors, *but solely in God.* This is what brings the blessing. If we *say* we trust in Him but in reality do not, then God taking us at our word, lets us see that we do not really confide in Him; and hence failure arises. On the other hand, if our trust in the Lord is real, help will surely come.

"According to your faith be it unto you" (Matthew 9:29). It is a source of deep sorrow to me, that, notwithstanding my having so many times before referred to this point, thereby to encourage believers in the Lord Jesus, to roll all their cares upon God, and to trust in Him at all times. Still by many it is put down to mere natural causes that I am helped; as if the Living God were no more the Living God, and as if in former ages answers to prayer might have been expected, but that in the nineteenth century they must not be looked for.

THE WILL OF GOD

How important it is to ascertain the will of God before we undertake anything, because we are then not only blessed in our own souls, but also the work of our hands will prosper. Just in as many points as we are acting according to the mind of God, in so many are we blessed and made a blessing. Our manner of living is according to the mind of the Lord, for He delights in seeing His children come to Him. Therefore, though I am weak and erring in many points, yet He blesses me in this particular.

First, to see that the work in which he desires to be engaged is *God's work*.

Second, that *he* is the person to be engaged in this work.

Third, that *God's time* is come, when he should do this work.

Fourth, and then to be assured that if he seeks God's help in His own appointed way, He will not fail him.

We have always found this to be true and expect to find it so again on the basis of the promises of God to the end of our course.

Be slow to take new steps in the Lord's service, or in your business, or in your families. Weigh everything well; weigh all in the light of the Holy Scriptures, and in the fear of God.

Seek to have no will of your own; in order to ascertain the mind of God, regarding any steps you propose to take, so that you can honestly say, you are willing to do the will of God, if He will only please to instruct you.

But when you have found out what the will of God

is, seek for His help, and seek it earnestly, perseveringly, patiently, believingly, and expectantly: and you will surely in His own time and way obtain it.

We do not have to rush forward in self-will and say, I will do the work, and I will trust the Lord for means, this cannot be real trust, it is the counterfeit of faith, it is presumption; and though God, in great pity and mercy, may even help us out of debt; it does on no account prove that we were right in going forward before His time was come. Rather, we ought to say to ourselves under these circumstances:

"Am I indeed doing *the work of God?*" And if so, *I* may not be the person to do it; or if I am the person, *His time* may not be now for me to go forward; it may be His good pleasure to exercise my faith and patience. Therefore, I ought to quietly to wait for His time; for when it is come, God will help. Acting on this principle brings blessing.

To ascertain the Lord's will we ought to use scriptural means. Prayer, the Word of God, and His Spirit should be united together. We should go to the Lord repeatedly in prayer, and ask Him to teach us by His Spirit through His Word. *I said by His Spirit through His word.* For if we think that His Spirit led us to do so and so, because certain facts are so and so, and yet His Word is opposed to the step that we are going to take, we will be deceiving ourselves. No situation, no business will be given to me by God, in which I have not time enough to care about my soul.

Therefore, however outward circumstances may appear, it can only be considered as permitted of God by proving the genuineness of my love, faith, and obedience by seeking His will. For by no means would I ever take a step contrary to His will.

MARRIAGE

To enter upon the marriage union is one of the most deeply important events of life. It cannot be too prayerfully treated. Our happiness, our usefulness, our living for God or for ourselves afterwards, are often most intimately connected with our choice. Therefore, this choice should be made in the most prayerful manner. Neither beauty, nor age, nor money, nor mental powers, should be that which prompts the decision; but much waiting upon God for guidance should be used.

A hearty purpose to be willing to be guided by Him should be aimed after.

True godliness without a shadow of doubt, should be the first and absolutely needful qualification to a Christian with regard to a companion for life.

In addition to this, however, it ought to be, at the same time, calmly and patiently weighed, whether there is suitableness in other respects. For instance, for an educated man to choose an entirely uneducated woman is unwise. For however much he might be willing to cover the defect by his love it will work very unhappily with regard to the children.

PRAYER AND ANSWERS TO PRAYER

I myself have been waiting for twenty-nine years for an answer to prayer concerning a certain spiritual blessing. Day by day I have been enabled to continue in prayer for this blessing. At home and abroad, in this country, in foreign lands, in health, in sickness, however much occupied, I have been enabled day by day by God's help to bring this matter before Him; and still I have not the full answer. Nevertheless, I look for it. I expect it confidently. The very fact that day after day, and year after year, for twenty-nine years, the Lord has enabled me to continue, patiently, and believingly to wait on Him for the blessing. This further encourages me to wait on. I am so fully assured that God hears me about this matter, that I have often been enabled to praise Him beforehand for the full answer, which I shall ultimately receive to my prayers on this subject. Thus, you see dear reader, that while I have hundreds, yes, thousands of answers, year by year, I have also, like yourself and other believers, the trial of faith concerning certain matters.

Anxiety Avoided by Prayer

Although all believers in the Lord Jesus are not called upon to establish orphan houses, schools for poor children, etc., and trust in God for their means; all believers, according to the will of God concerning them in Christ Jesus, may cast, and ought to cast all their care upon Him. Because He cares for them, and they need not be anxiously concerned about anything, as is plainly seen from 1 Peter 1:7; Philippians iv.6; Matthew 6:25-34.

My Lord is not limited; He can supply again, He knows that this present case has been sent to me; and thus this way of living far from *leading to anxiety* regarding possible future want, but rather the means of keeping from it. This way of living has often been the means of reviving the work of grace in my heart when I have been getting cold. It also has been the means of bringing me back again to the Lord, after I have been backsliding. For it will not do, and is impossible to live in sin, and at the same time be in communion with God, and to draw down from heaven everything one needs for the life that now is. Answer to prayer obtained in this way has been the means of quickening my soul, and filling me with much joy.

I met at a brother's house with several believers, when a sister said that she had often thought about the care and burden I must have on my mind, regarding the obtaining of the necessary supplies for so many persons. As this may not be a solitary instance, I would state that, by the grace of God, this is no cause of anxiety to me. Years ago I cast the children upon the Lord. The whole work is His, and it becomes me to be *without carefulness*. In whatever points I am lacking, in this point I am able by the grace of God, to roll the burden upon my heavenly Father.

Though now being, July 1845, for about seven years our funds have been so exhausted, that it has been comparatively a rare case that there have been means in hand to meet the necessities of the orphans for three days at a time. Yet, I have only once been tried in spirit, and that was on September 18, 1838, when for the first time the Lord seemed not to regard our prayer.

But when He did send help at that time, and I saw that it was only for the trial of our faith and not because He had forsaken the work that we were brought so low. My soul was strengthened and encouraged, and I have not allowed myself to distrust the Lord since that time, and I have not even been cast down when in the deepest poverty.

Nevertheless, in this respect I am as much as ever dependent on the Lord; and I earnestly beseech for myself and my fellow laborers the prayers of all those, to whom the glory of God is dear. How great would be the dishonor to the name of God, if we, who have so publicly made our boast in Him, would fail in our faith and act on these very points as the world does! Help us, then, brethren, with your prayers that we may trust in God to the end. We can expect nothing but that our faith will yet be tried, and it may be more than ever before. We shall fail if the Lord does not uphold us.

BORROWING AND PRAYING

As regards borrowing money, I have considered that there is no ground to go away from the door of the Lord to that of a believer, so long as He is willing to supply our need.

COMMUNION WITH GOD IN PRAYER

How truly precious it is that everyone who rests alone upon the Lord Jesus for salvation, has in the living God a Father to whom he may fully unburden himself concerning the most minute affairs of his life, and concerning everything that lies upon his heart! Dear reader, do you know the living God? Is He, in Jesus, your Father? Be assured that Christianity is something more than forms and creeds and ceremonies: there is life, and power, and reality, in our holy faith. If you never have known this, then come and taste for yourself. I beseech you affectionately to meditate and pray over the following verses: John 3:16; Romans 10:9-10; Acts 10:43; 1 John Verse 1.

CONDITIONS OF PRAYER

Go with all your own temporal and spiritual needs to the Lord. Bring also the necessities of your friends and relatives to the Lord. Do this and you will perceive how able and willing He is to help you. However, if you do not at once obtain answers to your prayers, be not discouraged; but continue patiently, believing, perseveringly to wait upon God. If what you have asked for would be for your real good, and therefore for the honor of the Lord; and as assuredly if you ask it solely on the ground of the worthiness of our Lord Jesus, so assuredly you will obtain the blessing. I myself have had to wait upon God concerning certain matters for years, before I obtained answers to my prayers; but at last they came. At this very time, I have still to renew my requests daily before God, respecting a certain blessing for which I have besought Him for over eleven years and which I have as yet obtained only in part, but I have no doubt that the full blessing will be granted in the end.

The great point is that we ask only for that which would

be for the glory of God to give to us; for that, and that alone will be for our real good. But it is not enough that the thing for which we ask God be for His honor and glory, but we must also ask it in the name of the Lord Jesus and expect it only on the ground of His merits and worthiness. Also we should believe that God is able and willing to give us what we ask Him for. We should continue in prayer until the blessing is granted; without fixing a time to God when, or the circumstances under which, He should give the answer. Patience should always be exercised in connection with our prayer. Lastly, we should, at the same time, look for and expect an answer until it comes. If we pray in this way, we shall not only have answers, thousands of answers to our prayers; but our own souls will be greatly refreshed and invigorated in connection with these answers.

If the obtaining of your requests were not for your real good, or were not tending to the honor of God, you might pray for a long time, without obtaining what you desire. The glory of God should be always before the children of God, in what they desire at His hands; and their own spiritual profit being so intimately connected with the honor of God should never be lost sight of in their petitions.

But now, suppose we are believers in the Lord Jesus, and make our requests unto God, depending alone on the Lord Jesus as the ground of having them granted; suppose also, that so far as we are able honestly and uprightly to judge, the obtaining of our requests would be for our real spiritual good and for the honor of God; lastly, we need to *continue* in prayer until the blessing is granted unto us. It is not enough to begin to pray, nor to pray aright; nor is it enough to continue *for a time* to pray; but we must patiently and believingly continue in prayer until we obtain an answer. Further, we have not only *to continue* in prayer unto the end, but we also have to *believe* that God does hear us, and will answer our prayers. Most frequently we fail *in not continuing* in prayer until the blessing is obtained and *in not expecting* the blessing.

FAITH, PRAYER, AND THE WORD OF GOD

Prayer and faith, the universal remedies against every want and every difficulty; and the nourishment of prayer and faith, and God's holy Word, helped me over all the difficulties.

It is now March of 1895, and I never remember a time in all my Christian walk of sixty-nine years and four months that I have not been directed rightly when I *sincerely* and *patiently* sought to know the will of God by the teaching of the Holy Ghost through the instrumentality of the Word of God. But if *honesty of heart* and *uprightness before God* were lacking, or if I did not *patiently* wait upon God for instruction, or preferred *the counsel of my fellow men* to the declarations of *the Word of the living God,* I made great mistakes.

SECRET PRAYER

Let none expect to have the mastery over his inward corruption in any degree, without going in his weakness again and again to the Lord for strength. Nor will prayer with others, or conversing with the brethren, make up for secret prayer.

SNARES OF SATAN REGARDING PRAYER

It is a common temptation of Satan to make us give up the reading of the Word and prayer when our enjoyment is gone; as if it were of no use to read the Scriptures when we do not enjoy them, and as if it were of no use to pray when we have no spirit of prayer. While the truth of the matter is, in order to enjoy the Word, we ought to continue to read it, and the way to obtain a spirit of prayer is to continue praying; for the less we read the Word of God, the less we desire to read it, and the less we pray, the less we desire to pray.

WORK AND PRAYER

Often the work of the Lord itself may be a temptation to keep us from that communion with Him that is so essential to the benefit of our own souls. Let no one think that public prayer will make up for close communion. Here is the great secret of success. Work with all your might; but trust not in the least in your work. Pray with all your might for the blessing of God; but work at the same time with all diligence, patience, and perseverance. Pray then, and work. Work and pray. Again, pray and then work...and so on all the days of your life. The result will surely be, abundant blessing. Whether you see much fruit or little fruit, *such* kind of service will be blessed. Speak also for the Lord as if everything depended on your exertions; yet trust not the least in your exertions, but in the Lord, who alone can cause your efforts to be made effectual, and to the benefit of your fellow men or fellow believers. Remember, God delights to bestow blessing as the result of earnest, believing prayer.

PREACHING

It came immediately to my mind that such sort of preaching might do for illiterate country people, but that it would never do before a well-educated assembly in town. I thought the truth ought to be preached at all costs, however, it ought to be given in a different form, suited to the hearers. Thus I remained unsettled in my mind as it regards the mode of preaching; and it is not surprising that I did see the truth concerning this matter, for I did not understand the work of the Spirit, and therefore I did not see the powerlessness of human eloquence. Furthermore, I did not keep in mind that if the most illiterate persons in the congregation can comprehend the discourse, the most educated will understand it too; but that the reverse does not hold true.

RESTITUTION

Restitution is the revealed will of God. If it is omitted, while we have it in our power to make it, guilt remains in the conscience, and spiritual progress is hindered. Even though it might be connected with difficulty, self-denial, and great loss, it is to be attended to. If the persons who have been defrauded are dead, their heirs are to be found out, if this can be done, and restitution is to be made to them. But there may be cases when this cannot be done, and then only, the money should be given to the Lord for His work or His poor. One more word. About fifty years ago, I knew a man under concern about his soul, who had defrauded his master of two sacks of flour, and who was urged by me to confess this sin to his late employer, and to make restitution. However, he would not do it, and the result was that for twenty years he never obtained real peace of soul until the thing was done.

REWARDS

Christians do not always remember that while we are saved by grace, and only by grace, that in the matter of salvation works are altogether excluded. Yet so far as the rewards of grace are concerned, in the world to come there is an intimate connection between the life of the Christian here and the enjoyment and the glory in the day of Christ's appearing.

SIN AND SALVATION

Humbling ourselves lasts our whole life. Jesus came not to save *painted* but *real* sinners; but He *has* saved us, and will surely make it manifest.

SPIRIT OF GOD

At Stuttgart, the dear brethren had been entirely uninstructed about the truths relating to the power and presence of the Holy Ghost in the Church of God, and to our ministering one to another as fellow members in the Body of Christ. I had known enough by painful consequences when brethren began to meet professedly in dependence upon the Holy Spirit without knowing what was meant by it, and thus meetings had become opportunities *for unprofitable talking rather than for godly edifying.* All these matters ought to be left to the ordering of the Holy Ghost, and if it had been truly good for them, the Lord would have not only led me to speak *at that time,* but also on *the very subject* on which they desired that I should speak to them.

TRUTH

Whenever particular truths in the Word of God are emphasized as one being more important than another, even if they are the most precious truths connected with our being risen in Christ, or our heavenly calling, or prophecy, sooner or later those who emphasize *these particular truths,* and make them too prominent, will be losers in their own souls, and, if they are teachers they will injure those whom they teach.

UNIVERSALISM

In reference to universal salvation, I found that they had been led into this error because:

(1) They did not see the difference between the earthly calling of the Jews and the heavenly calling of the believers in the Lord Jesus in the present dispensation, and therefore they said that, because the words "everlasting," etc., are applied to "the possession of the land of Canaan" and the "priesthood of Aaron," therefore, the punishment of the wicked cannot be without end, seeing that the possession

of Canaan and the priesthood of Aaron are not without end. My endeavor, therefore, was to show the brethren the difference between the *earthly* calling of Israel and our *heavenly* one, and to prove from Scripture that, whenever the word "everlasting" is used with reference to things purely not of the Earth, but beyond time, it denotes a period without end.

(2) They had laid exceeding great stress upon a few passages where, in Luther's translation of the German Bible, the word hell occurs, and where it ought to have been translated either "Hades" in some passages, or "grave" in others, and where they saw a *deliverance out of hell,* and a *being brought up out of hell,* instead of *"out of the grave."*

WORD OF GOD

The Word of God is our only standard, and the Holy Spirit our only teacher. In addition to the Holy Bible, which should always be *"The Book,"* and the most important book to us not only in theory but also in practice, such like books seem to me the most useful for the growth of the inner man. Yet one has to be cautious in the choice, and to guard against reading too much.

WORK FOR GOD

When God orders something to be done for the glory of His name, He is both able and willing to find the needed individuals for the work and the means required. Thus, when the Tabernacle in the Wilderness was to be erected, He not only fitted men for the work, but He also touched the hearts of the Israelites to bring the necessary materials of gold, silver, and precious stones; and all these things were not only brought, but in such abundance that a proclamation had to be made in the camp that no more articles should be brought because there were more than enough. And again, when God for the praise of His name had Solomon build Him the Temple, He provided such an amount of gold, silver, precious stones, brass, iron, etc., for it, that all the palaces or temples that have been built since are insignificant in comparison.

STUDY GUIDE

BIOGRAPHY

HIS CHILDHOOD

1. What is the name of the town and country where George Müeller was born?

2. What is that country called today?

3. Describe the childhood of George Müeller.

HIS NEW BIRTH

1. What was the turning point in George Müeller's life and destiny and where did it occur?

2. What was the first thing he did when he returned to his room that evening?

3. What peaked his interest in the Mission Field?

4. What was the response to George Müeller's first sermon in the tiny chapel where he went to aid the elderly pastor?

5. How did God help him when he was asked to preach again in the afternoon?

6. What effect did this have on his manner of preaching?

NEW PATHWAYS

1. What seed was planted in George Müeller's mind after reading the Life Story of A.H. Francke?

2. Name a few of the worldly things that were gone from Müeller's life while in the hand of God on the Potter's Wheel.

PASTORAL WORK AND MARRIAGE

1. What role did "pew rents" play in Müeller's decision regarding a salary?

2. How did he meet his future wife, Miss Mary Groves?

3. What decision did they make early in their marriage regarding earthly possessions.

4. List the seven important experiences that molded George Müeller's ministry.

5. What are the three things listed in Joshua 1:8 regarding 'true prosperity'?

GROWTH IN GOD'S WORD

1. What were the three chief reasons that Müeller wrote for establishing an orphan home?

2. What important omission did he make when asking God to supply the means for the orphan home?

3. Among the first givers of gifts to the Orphan Home was a poor, sickly, seamstress. Why did Müeller use her example as a foundation of giving for the orphan ministry?

4. How did Mr. Müeller respond to the neighbors close by the newly proposed Orphan Home Number 3?

5. What Scripture reference did he base his response on?

THE WORD OF GOD AND PRAYER

1. List the three men whose biographies influenced George Müeller's life and ministry.

2. People often asked him the secret of his peace when being responsible for so many orphans and workers. How did he respond?

3. What happened when Müeller tried to lay away a few funds for another time?

4. List the two reasons he gave for never doing it again. Fill in the blanks:

First, he must go into no byways or paths of his own for a ----------out of a----.

Second, that in proportion as he had been ---------to honor God and bring some -----to His name by trusting Him, he was in ------of dishonoring Him.

5. What is a Gordion Knot?

6. What Scripture reference did Müeller use as a basis for praying by pleading with God by Holy Arguments?

7. When asked the secret of his life of service he said: "There was a day that I ----, utterly ----.

8. A few hours after the death of his wife, George Müeller went to a prayer meeting and spoke these words; "Beloved brethren and sisters in Christ, I ask you to join with me in hearty ------ and ------------to my precious Lord for His loving kindness in having taken my darling, beloved wife out of the pain and suffering which she has endured, into His own presence, and as I rejoice in ------------- that is for her happiness. So I now rejoice as I realize how far happier she is in --------her Lord, whom she loved so well, than in any joy she has known or could know here. I ask you also to pray that the Lord will so enable me to have ---------- in her joy that my bereaved heart may be occupied with her blessedness instead of my ----------loss."

ANSWERS TO PRAYER

HOW TO ASCERTAIN THE WILL OF GOD

1. George Müeller listed six ways to find the will of God, what was number 5?

2. What Scripture did the Lord bring to George Müeller's mind when he wanted to know how to pray for all the necessary funds etc for the orphan homes? Fill in the blanks: "Open thy -----wide, and I will ----it."

3. In 1841, there came a day when yearly reports would

be written up and distributed to the public, however, a decision was made to hold the reports for a period of time. What was the reason?

4. In November of 1857, the boiler in Orphan House Number 1 began leaking badly and there were 300 children and babies in that home. How did God answer prayer during this crisis?

5. Of the thousands of answers to prayer that George Müeller received you can give glory to the Lord by reading them to others or better yet commit one or two to memory and share them as the Lord leads.

6. On June 7, 1884, George Müeller received the largest legacy ever received during his time of ministry. What was the sum of it?

GLOSSARY

A.H.Francké: Established orphan homes in Halle one hundred years prior to Müeller. His biography had a large impact on Müeller's decision to also establish orphanages.

Another example of holy argument is the Samaritan woman arguing with Jesus regarding the children's bread in Matthew 15:26-28.

Bethesda Chapel: A chapel in Bristol pastored by both Mr. Craik and Mr. Müeller.

Boiler: Part of a heating apparatus that produced the steam to heat the Orphan Homes.

Ebenezer Chapel: A small chapel in Teignmouth that Müeller pastored.

George Whitfield: A well-known English preacher who helped spread the Great Awakening in Britain. Further information is available on his life in a book compiled by Ray Comfort called "Whitfield Gold" published and available through Bridge Logos at www.bridgelogos.com or by calling 800-631-5802.

Gordian Knot: A legendary knot tied by King Gordius of Phyrgia and cut by Alexander the Great with his sword after hearing the oracle promise that whoever could undo it would become the next ruler of Asia.

Halberstadt: A town in Prussia.

Holy Argument: Pleading with God by using holy argument in prayer. Putting a cause before God as an advocate would plead before a judge. Christ Jesus is our advocate with God. *"My little children, these things write I unto you, that ye sin not. And if any man sin, we have an advocate with the Father, Jesus Christ the righteous"* (1 John 2:1).

Hudson Taylor: Missionary and Evangelist in the China Inland Mission.

Importunity: Importunity is persistence in prayer. Example: The Widow and the Unjust Judge. (See Luke 18:5-7.)

Jehovah Jireh: The Lord our Provider or the Lord will provide.

John Newton: An English sailor and clergyman. He authored the hymn Amazing Grace. Further information on him is available in the Pure Gold Classic called "The Amazing Works of John Newton" published by Bridge Logos and available on www.bridgelogos.com or by called 800-631-5802.

Kroppenstaedt: A town in Prussia.

Martin Luther: Professor of Theology and more importantly a prominent figure in the Protestant Reformation and regarding salvation by Grace.

Pecuniary Aid: Financial aid.

Pew Rentals: A practice of receiving monies from the rental of pews to persons in the congregation probably participated in by the more affluent. A practice George Müeller found distasteful and unscriptural.

Prussia: Now called Germany.

The Fly: A horse-drawn carriage.

The Scriptural Knowledge Institution for Home and Abroad: Established by George Müeller for the purpose of schooling children and adults in the Word of God in total dependence upon God for all necessities.

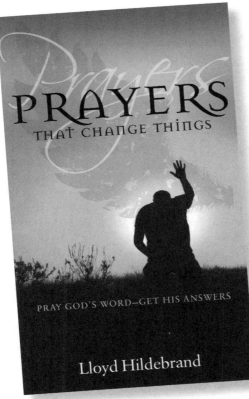

Prayers That Change Things
Pray God's Word— Get His Answers
by Lloyd Hildebrand

*P*rayers That Change Things is a new book by an established writer of books on prayer, Lloyd B. Hildebrand, who co-authored the very popular *Prayers That Prevail* series, *Bible Prayers for All Your Needs*, *Praying the Psalms*, *Healing Prayers*, and several others. This new book contains prayers about personal feelings and situations, prayers that are built directly from the Bible. The reader will discover that praying the Scriptures will truly bring about changes to so many things, especially their outlook on life and the circumstances of life. These life-imparting, life-generating, life-giving, and life-sustaining prayers are sure to bring God's answers to meet the believer's needs. Pray them from your heart; then wait for God to speak to you. Remember, He always speaks through His Word.

This revolutionary approach joins the power of prayer with the power of God's Word.

ISBN: 978-1-61036-105-7
MM / 192 pages

"The Consummate Apologetics Bible...

Everything you ever need to share your faith."

"The Evidence Bible is the reservoir overflowing with everything evangelistic—powerful quotes from famous people, amazing anecdotes, sobering last words, informative charts, and a wealth of irrefutable evidence to equip, encourage, and enlighten you, like nothing else.

I couldn't recommend it more highly."

– Kirk Cameron

Compiled by Ray Comfort

This edition of *The Evidence Bible* includes notes, commentaries, and quotations that make it a comprehensive work of apologetics and evangelism that will be helpful to every believer. It covers a variety of practical topics, including the following:

- How to answer objections to Christianity
- How to talk about Christ with people of other religions
- How to counter evolutionary theories, while providing evidence for God's creation
- How to grow in Christ
- How to use the Ten Commandments when witnessing

There is no other Bible like this one. Every soul-winner who wants to lead others to Christ will want a copy of *The Evidence Bible*, because it provides springboards for preaching and witnessing, shares insights from well-known Christian leaders, gives points for open-air preaching, reveals the scientific facts contained within the Bible, and supplies the believer with helpful keys to sharing one's faith. The Bible is "the sword of the Spirit," and this edition of the Bible will motivate believers to become true spiritual warriors in their daily interactions with others.

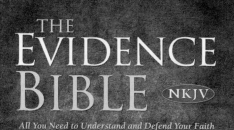

ISBN: 9780882705255
PB

Also available in duo tone leather.

ISBN: 9780882708973

Bridge Logos

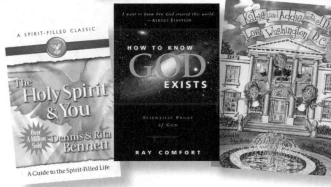

Top 20

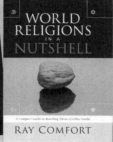

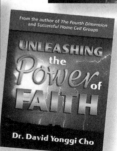

Pure Gold Classics
Timeless Truth in a Distinctive, Best-Selling Collection

- Illustrations
- Detailed index
- Author biography
- In-depth Bible study
- Expanding Collection—40-plus titles
- Sensitively Revised in Modern English

AN EXPANDING COLLECTION
OF THE BEST-LOVED
CHRISTIAN CLASSICS
OF ALL TIME.

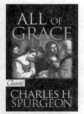

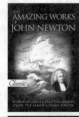

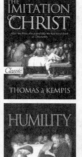
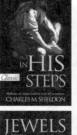
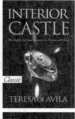

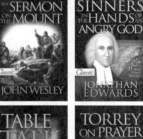
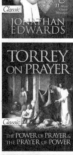
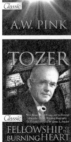

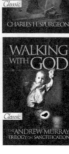